San Juan

THE AMERICAS

Series Editors:

ILAN STAVANS and IRENE VILAR

■

Advisory Board:

Homero Aridjis

Ariel Dorfman

Rosario Ferré

Jean Franco

Alvaro Mutis

Mirta Ojito

Margaret Sayers Peden

Luis J. Rodriguez

Bob Shacochis

Antonio Skármeta

Doug Unger

San Juan

Memoir of a City

Edgardo Rodríguez Juliá

Translated by
Peter Grandbois

Foreword by
Antonio Skármeta

The University of Wisconsin Press

The University of Wisconsin Press
1930 Monroe Street, 3rd Floor
Madison, Wisconsin 53711-2059

www.wisc.edu/wisconsinpress/

3 Henrietta Street
London WC2E 8LU, England

Originally published as *San Juan: Ciudad Soñada*
© 2005 Edgardo Rodríguez Juliá

1   3   5   4   2

Printed in the United States of America

Library of Congress Cataloging-in-Publication Data
Rodríguez Juliá, Edgardo, 1946–
[San Juan, ciudad soñada. English]
San Juan: memoir of a city / Edgardo Rodríguez Juliá;
translated by Peter Grandbois;
foreword by Antonio Skármeta.
p.   cm.—(The Americas)
Includes bibliographical references.
ISBN 0-299-20370-0 (cloth: alk. paper)
ISBN 0-299-20374-3 (pbk.: alk. paper)
1. San Juan (P.R.)—Description and travel.
2. Rodríguez Juliá, Edgardo, 1946-—Homes and
haunts—Puerto Rico—San Juan.
3. San Juan (P.R.)—In literature.   I. Title.
F1981.S2R56913   2007
917.295′1—dc22   2006031485

For

SAMUEL APONTE,

connoisseur of memorable cities

Real cities have something else, some individual bony structure under the muck. Los Angeles has Hollywood—and hates it. It ought to consider itself lucky. Without Hollywood it would be a mail-order city. Everything in the catalogue you could get better somewhere else.

Raymond Chandler, *The Little Sister*

I lived in the literal L.A. and dreamed my own private L.A.

James Ellroy, *Crime Wave*

Changed to a light shirt, I walk out to Cervantes Street. Shadow-barred. A water sprinkler or a tank approaches. The corners are empty. The boulevards open like novels waiting to be written. Clouds like the beginnings of stories.

Derek Walcott, "Tropic Zone"

I sat on the bed and drank the bottle of champagne. I felt melancholy, so I decided to go swimming. I drove out to Luisa Aldea where the beach was empty.

Hunter S. Thompson, *The Rum Diary*

San Juan no existe porque no posee aún sus palabras, porque su población no tiene aún su literatura.

Eduardo Lalo, *Los pies de San Juan*

Contents

Contents

Maps

COURTESY OF U.S. GEOLOGICAL SURVEY

Foreword

A Dream Realized

ANTONIO SKÁRMETA

Please, let us immediately abandon the idea that in this book we are going to encounter a lyric undercurrent trilling with touristic deceit in order to exalt the beauty of an island. Edgardo Rodríguez Juliá knows too much about Puerto Rico to succumb to such banalities. His is another road. The city and his biography become united. Each place the poet names—a palace, cathedral, hospital, tavern, or brothel—forms a scene placed in the narrative not simply as a catalogue but as a space where we uncover a piece of the poet's life in every hue—melancholy, bliss, love, jazz, politics, bohemianism, or literature. It is astonishing how frank and spontaneous the author is in telling his tale: to live in the city and to watch how he lives.

Let us not delay in talking of the fact that this book is not simply a separate chapter in the narrative of one of the greatest writers in the Caribbean, but is instead a text that links together all the marvels of his novelistic work. In *La noche oscura del Niño Avilés* and *La renuncia del héroe Baltasar* he submerged himself in eighteenth-century Puerto Rico in search of the roots of his town's identity without any ambition toward historical pedantry. But now his vision of San Juan in this century is full of a history shared as much by the city as by the author's imagination.

The search for an identity so profound, tinted by the peculiar situation of a country in transit between so many races and cultures, has provided Rodríguez Juliá with the greatest ability a writer can desire: to be both cultured and intuitive. This is not a book that can be catalogued in the geography section of the library. Instead, it should be filed with the narratives or, better yet, the biographies.

The distinguished narrator has made an elegant pirouette through civic as well as personal history: by giving us the tale of his city, he has allowed himself such intimacy that he simultaneously narrates for us the biography of San Juan as well as his own. Still, I note immediately that in a town that cultivates intimate ties among its people, a biography is not just a compilation of magnificent exploits or quotidian details from an individual author's life but rather takes the historical temperature of generations: his fellow writers, his painter friends, the practitioners of politics, the great foreign masters like Pedro Salinas or Pablo Casals, who lived the perplexing beauty of an inspirational landscape, easing their sadness for lost lands.

San Juan and its neighboring cities do not escape the fate of a destructive modernity that not only erases walls, street lights, and plazas, but also bars, those cherished treasures whose wounds remain throbbing in the memory of the older generations who, in a frenzy of articulation, can dream of a city and make it as exciting as a Hollywood production. Suddenly, at the change of the traffic light appears Toño Machuca, the protagonist from the novel *Mujer con sombrero Panamá*, who has run into a key point in the new social geography: "They kidnapped Toño Machuca there because his secret life was a contradiction between perverse appetites and bourgeois respectability."

What precision Rodríguez Juliá shows by nailing down in one judgment the game, or the favorite drama of so many Latin American cities! The struggle between order and chaos. Between security and adventure. Between desire and frustration. The anguish of millions to cross over the border: *to cross the line.*

That is why it is not strange that authors surface in this book, evoked not simply as pencil marks secondary to the main tale but essential brushstrokes that paint the road through history: "Olga Nolla places us in spaces of amorous secrets and clandestine correspondences, where, like the streets of Miramar, the lives of high-class women are necessarily hidden in existential discretion."

The *boricua* writer feels himself a man in his context. If he takes a step in one direction, he knows that around the corner there are tracks that remain unexplored, and, sooner or later, he will find the road to justice, not necessarily justice for everyone but for that part of everyone that is the space we have lived together emotionally. Even the smallest part of this text evokes a space and a sense that both exceeds and enriches.

This San Juan of the great Caribbean writer is an event, which in the far seeing eye of the tale melts and recasts the architecture with the style of lives that nourish the city's streets and homes. And so, when we enter the old quarter, these are the nuptials that are celebrated: "of lives led in proximity, of indiscretions veiled by shutters, of rumors heard through partition walls and in entryways."

I very much doubt that a pedestrian in San Juan would not enrich his understanding of the city through the evocation of these lines. Rodríguez Juliá's book is a marvel of description, but at the same time, it is a parade of explosive images conveying atmosphere, microclimates, and upheavals, which cities do not reveal upon first encounter.

And let's not forget the title [*San Juan: Ciudad Soñada,* as it appeared in the original edition], for it alludes to the surreal side each city offers us; to the undeniable dreams the city inspires in its artists, the same ones who curse her, ignore her, or exalt her; to those who left the island in search of other dreams that the island's precariousness would not allow, and who return years later. As Luis Rafael Sánchez would say, "Don't cry for us, Puerto Rico." From above, one can see the curves of the Puerto Rican coastline with its stubborn blueness, a blue that adorns itself with green whenever it feels like it. And, when descending from the plane, the impatience to arrive excites the passengers, and the recognition of these familiar places explodes happily along the length and width of the aircraft. What a variety of life's flavors are contained in a wisdom that cannot be explained!

The city is imagined with respect to the autonomy of a poet who sees the transfiguration of the neighborhoods, the internal or external migrations, but who remains faithful to the code he inherits from Baudelaire in "Las Nubes": to search for inverted cities hanging from the sky. The neurasthenia of light, the certainty of imagination. The inspiration rests on reality but also upon dreams and universal nightmares: the Fellini of the *Satyricon;* Piranesi's engravings; jazz music; the cover of a Miles Davis album; Palés Matos's arrival at the capital; the bohemianism of René Marqués, Rafael Tufiño, and Tuti Umpierre; the singer Sylvia Rexach.

A city, and Rodríguez Juliá expresses this beautifully, is also that which it is not, that which it can never be; in the picaresque manner it deforms and makes ironic whatever it is forced to be or the shameful limitations of the foreign model that strangles it. The imagined city. The Paseo La Princesa was conceived according to the bourgeois aspirations of the avenues in Madrid, which themselves dreamed of faraway Parisian avenues. The city made its own precious reality from the remnants of those dreams.

The imagined city spills forth—no less insightful for its intensity—in the presence of the narrators of San Juan: V. S. Naipaul and his first step from the Caribbean and Trinidad to England, Rosario Ferré and *La casa de la laguna,* Pedro Salinas with his great poem "El Contemplado," or the verses of Derek Walcott, whose poetic ecstasy in San Juan "is a meditation over ancestral memory." But he also explores scenes with Manolo, the detective from *Sol de medianoche,* perhaps the most intense of Rodríguez Juliá's books: "A mystery novel where the detective is a type of 'beach bum' with a catholic education? . . . I think that Isla Verde is the most suitable neighborhood for the private detective to plan his strategy for the search that will ultimately reveal the character of the city. Just as the sea surprises us because it is never the same, the city leaves us perplexed. Its many faces hide its heart, its character."

There is nothing more to say. This great Latin American writer, this superb swimmer who speaks tirelessly about the beach, this scholar of sophisticated literature and expert in nightclub music from the *boites,* this aficionado who celebrates a good poem the same way he does a home run in a baseball game has taken us through San Juan and its environs. He has done it and continues to do it from the beginning, riding on the biography of his childhood, youth, and adulthood, taking note of the milestones and, with a calm, clear gaze, attentive to what his colleagues wrote and lived but more so to what he dreamed and continues dreaming.

San Juan is the imagined or dreamed city, a city that needs to be continually reinvented and does not lack for poets, painters, architects, and musicians who undertake the tour of its alleys and avenues with joyful spontaneity. It will not find its identity lying in the street. Its identity emerges each time its people walk its streets.

I write these final lines with impatience for it is now the reader will enter into Rodríguez Juliá's indispensable text.

San Juan

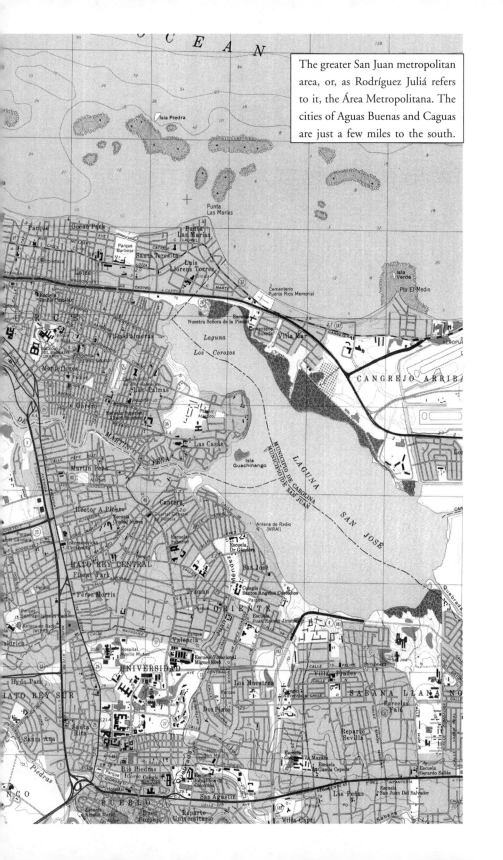

The greater San Juan metropolitan area, or, as Rodríguez Juliá refers to it, the Área Metropolitana. The cities of Aguas Buenas and Caguas are just a few miles to the south.

1

Ubi Sunt

The landscape of my childhood has disappeared and also that of my adolescence. In Puerto Rico, life is not simply cruel, it is also busy erasing our tracks, our footprints, besieging our memory. The first tyranny is part of the human condition, the second is a passion uniquely Puerto Rican.

The house I grew up in facing the Plaza de Aguas Buenas, now rechristened—take a guess—the "Plaza Luis A. Ferré," disappeared in the seventies. That house—with its corrugated tin roof and the long gallery we called *el martillo* (the hammer), the downstairs of which was occupied or not depending upon our business fortunes and the whims of my grandmother Ruperta, and the second floor dedicated to our living quarters, with the ausubo posts and the elegant wooden framework, and the roof that had to be replaced because of the Santa Clara winds—all of it was destroyed by the time Fania salsa was born at the Cheetah Club in New York.

The road from Aguas Buenas to Caguas, one of the most beautiful in the country, shaded by the thick canopy of flamboyanes and jacaranda trees as you travel from town to town, has also disappeared. I particularly loved driving up and down that hilly road—the genital, almost sexual, sensation of it—and the anticipation of glimpsing the mirages, the images of rivers, creeks and lagoons flowing over the

5

pavement. Originally, sugar cane covered the countryside; in the sixties, cattle grazed on the land. My mother—who knew everything about birds—would tell me of the friendship between the herons and the cattle. Today, after passing what was once called *la cantera* (the quarry), we recognize, in the distant Valley of Turabo, a housing development built by Levitt & Sons that reaches almost to Caguas. Time's wounds run deep through the landscape of my youth. A four-lane highway stretches across the land like an elongated basketball court, replacing the old road and its canopy of flamboyanes. It is unlikely the traffic between Aguas Buenas and Caguas merited such an autobahn. The narrow, little bridge spanning the ravine in La Union is also gone. Whenever I crossed it, I knew that I was near Aguas Buenas or Caguas, depending on which way I was going. In the twenties, the bridge did not yet exist. The few cars—one of them my grandfather's—traveling between the two towns crossed over dried riverbeds, and during the rising of the river, the people from Aguas Buenas were reminded of their nickname, "The Cripples," as they were cut off from Caguas and didn't attempt to cross the Cañaboncito River. My mother would tell me all this on our way to Caguas, as her humor improved the closer to town we got. The new bridge, a gargantuan structure, has pillars designed to withstand a flood the size of the Danube.

In Caguas, the Plaza Gautier Benítez, the Art Deco movie house, and the Teatro Alcázar still stand. Even the gothic-style parish, the Notre Dame School, and the Ildefonso Solá Morales Park, where Victor Pellot Power ("Vic Power") ruled over first base, are little changed. In 1955, when I was living in Aguas Buenas, Caguas was my Paris, the road between the two towns my Champs Elysées. Sometimes, in the afternoon, my mother celebrated the days she felt free from the grip of oncophobia by treating me to a banana split at the only diner in Caguas's plaza. We would go by *carro público*.

Not long after, we moved to the avenue of "Progress." It was 1957, and I was eleven. My father, always optimistic and heedless of the dark warnings of my neurasthenic mother, bought a house for

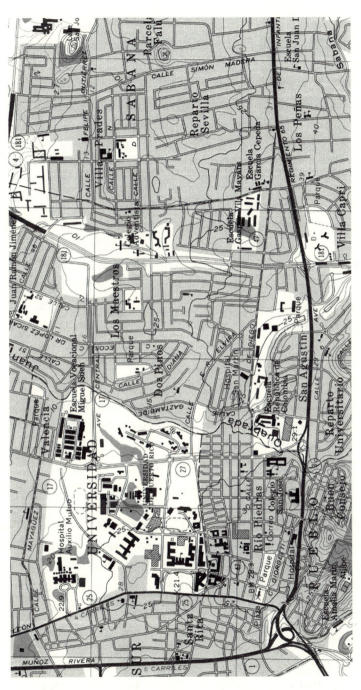

The southeastern section of greater San Juan. Notice that Avenida 65 de Infantería runs along the southern border of the map and has a slightly different name: Avenida Regimiento 65 de Infantería. Rodríguez Juliá grew up in a neighborhood between San Augustín and Villa Capri. Calle de Diego, the other street that is important to Rodríguez Juliá's youth, runs east to west through Río Piedras, connecting with Avenida 65 de Infantería on its western end. As Rodríguez Juliá mentions, El Jíbarito Bar and Grill sits on the corner of de Diego and Ramón B. López, which is called Calle E. R. Elvira on this map. The Río Piedras campus of the University of Puerto Rico dominates the upper portion of the map.

eighteen thousand dollars on Avenida 65 de Infantería. There was
little traffic, then. Cars passed so infrequently that on weeknights
we played baseball and hide-and-seek in the avenue. My father assured us that they would build a frontage road in front of the house
to distance us from the deafening road noise when the traffic in-
creased in the years to come. Our home would once again face a
quiet street. "It is already in the works," he would say. In any case,
the house would appreciate more on the avenue. The "progress" my
father believed in demanded such sacrifices from us. My mother's
peasant mistrust suspected that such a road would never be built. So
it was that our house remained without the famous frontage road,
and we lived on the bank of an uncontrollable, savage Progress, a
deafening river of cars. And the nights of my asthmatic childhood
were assailed by horrific accidents in which gas tanks would explode
practically under my window. My mother said that my father had
never made a good deal in his life. Today that house is gone. In its
place, and stretching almost to the stoplight on the Expreso Trujillo
Alto, is Toñito's Auto Parts, specializing in Mazdas. The street running behind this tiny development, called "el Alamein" because it
was built after World War II, is still a middle-class residential street,
as it was in the fifties. My mother wanted my father to buy a house
on that street, probably because she was raised in a small town
where the shutters from her balcony opened to the life outside. I
lived in that house with the promise of the frontage road until I was
twenty-two.

From my new Champs Elysées on the 65 de Infantería, only the
south and east sides of the San José Preparatory School I once attended are now visible, rising above the Buen Consejo neighborhood. The noble building in which I studied was designed by Rafael
Carmoega, an unjustly forgotten Puerto Rican architect. The 65th
Infantry Shopping Center is also still there; in 1957 it had a huge sign
that, in keeping with the optimism of the time, proclaimed, *Todos*.
The houses that once lined the avenue—still awaiting that quiet
frontage road—are now businesses with such a proliferation of signs

that they cancel one another out in their quest for recognition. The old monument to the 65th Infantry Regiment has also disappeared, leaving in its place a statue of a Puerto Rican soldier wearing a winter cloak in the rugged mountains of Korea. The old monument was simple, sober, minimalist, and modern—the bronze cross of Malta in relief, framed in cement. The present one is extravagant, rhetorical, and grotesque in its realism. The original was erected two years after the war, the new one fifty years later. A little higher up, at the traffic light where McDonald's now sits, there used to be a place called Lugo's, where Papo Newman became a man. After all, the Avenida 65 de Infantería was *our* street.

I live in Guaynabo now. Let's just say my life arced through the University of Puerto Rico and Calle de Diego in the Sabana Llana sector. The University remains, as do the Río Piedras town plaza and the Green Village Condominiums, where I lived for thirty-one years. From my terrace here in Guaynabo, just before dawn, I gaze out at the hills of Jagüeyes and Bayamoncito. It is as if time has reversed, for alongside the walk-up where I live, the Peñagarícano family refuses to sell, stopping the construction of another new and more expensive housing project. They continue to breed cocks, both *mañaneros* and *vespertinos,* which crow all day.

From my vantage point, overlooking the hills of Guaynabo and Aguas Buenas, I have a view of the thick forest of palms and *meaítos,* an African tree that my mother oddly called *bucayos.* In this forest preserve hemmed in by the suburban landscape, in the trees that almost reach the railing of my balcony, live four magnificent macaws. I don't know whether they are Puerto Rican or exotic. *Anyway,* as the blondes of Guaynabo say, the birds make quite a fuss when they take flight and are often seen in Torrimar and Garden Hills.

Further down, next to the Peñagarícano family, lived the famous jurist, Don José Trías Monje. His ancestral home, with its swimming pool, has disappeared. As a university student, I used to visit that house, where his son, Arturo Trías, and I discussed poetry and

literature. In that area today, they've constructed a walk-up ambitiously named Granada Park.

Though few believe it, Guaynabo has always conjured the literary. José Luis González spent his childhood and adolescence near
where I live on the Martínez Nadal Expressway, where the Bellas
Artes Center sits today. I know this because in his book *La luna no
era de queso,* the first volume of his incomplete memoirs and one
of the best autobiographical novels in Puerto Rican literature, José
Luis mentions that he lived very close to the rural residence of Rafael Martínez Nadal. He describes the breeding of the pro statehood
leader's fighting cocks, and tells us how he once saw the drunken figure of a young poet arrive at that house, a dabbler in politics who
wore a filthy suit and kept his cotton pants up with either a necktie
or a rope. Always a good narrator, José Luis concludes that section of
his memoir with a description of this eccentric, well-bred youth who
by 1940 would transform the country. He never mentions the man's
name, identifying him only by his appearance. From the topic of the
criollo, cock-breeding Republican, we move to the "Petit Yankeeism"
à la Disney World of the Guaynabo mayor, Hector O'Neill, a man
who doesn't understand much English besides the "Yield" and "One
Way" signs that decorate Guaynabo, city of five stars!

In 1933 Don Rafael Martínez Nadal signed into law what in Governor Gore's time had been relegated to back alleys, and suddenly
cockfighting was once again legal in Puerto Rico. The cockfighting
club Canta Gallo was built alongside Martínez Nadal's house on the
outskirts of Guaynabo, the law signed with a feather pen taken from
Martínez Nadal's own illustrious rooster, Justicia. As always with
him, it was an irascible act.

As we travel today across San Juan in the northbound lanes, approaching the Bellas Artes Center, we see Martínez Nadal's house on
the left-hand side of the expressway that bears his name, opposite the
enormous parking lot for Kmart and Ruby Tuesday. The house has
no distinguishing characteristics, except that it is painted white and
blue, the colors of his party (the PNP), and indeed it may not be the

same one that José Luis knew in his adolescence. It looks like a house from the fifties or sixties, built on the site of the ancestral home. Viaducts and expressways, the many intersections and frontage roads, always render history invisible. Only while walking can memory glean fragments of the past; the speeding car is the enemy of remembrance.

The walk-up where I live is named Lincoln Park. It is located on the site of the old Lincoln Military Academy, which was founded by the infamous Colonel Valdés, self-proclaimed expert in space flight and honorary member of NASA. According to a friend who grew up near here, this area was known as Cuatro Calles because a stretch of the old Bayamón-Guaynabo highway, now Route 833, intersected with the highway to Los Filtros at the foot of the hill called, not surprisingly perhaps, La Lomita. Los Filtros was a filtration plant run by the Aqueducts and Sewer Authority during the forties. Back then it must have been very much on the outskirts of the metropolitan area, at the top of the hill nearest to Guaynabo. You had a view from there of San Juan's coastal plain to the north and of a much more rural Guaynabo than today to the south. It was our Mulholland Drive: the place where we could look out over the growing anthill of lights extending outward from the city below. At the foot of La Lomita district, there is a parking area with a railing made of pipe. I wonder if it was originally conceived as an observation point, a rest stop with a panoramic view. Today, the local truckers stop there to wash and wax their vehicles. On clear days, from the heights of La Lomita, you can glimpse the Capitol and El Morro, Isla Verde beach, Ocean Park, Condado, and Luis Muñoz Marín International Airport. Atop La Lomita sits an abandoned house. Here the view is nearly three hundred and sixty degrees, encompassing San Juan as well as the hills of Guaynabo and Aguas Buenas. The house is boarded up. It was the site of a tragedy. Someone told me it was a suicide, such a profoundly inward act that the beauty of the country can never make up for it. The tragedy of that house would fill a novel.

If the viaducts and expressways prevail, everything will become a frontage road, but not quite like the quiet road my mother wanted, rather that uncomfortable place no one pays attention to. It all becomes phantasmal, set at an angle difficult for the motorist to see. The urgency of the absence assaults us until we slow down. Only on foot can we once again feel its presence.

Where is the little house Juan Antonio Corretjer lived in? In 1966 I visited it for the first time with José María Bulnes. I was young and eager to know the history of Puerto Rican nationalism, honored to meet our national poet. As I remember now, that musty house was right across from the Club Caborrojeño. Constructed in the middle of the forest, the house had sunk somewhat into the hillside. Its tiny terrace, furnished with straw rocking chairs, made it slightly more modest than the house of that other bard from Trujillo Alto, Luis Muñoz Marín.

With my wife, Ilca, driving me, I searched along the stretch of the road that runs from Guaynabo to La Muda but found no sign of the place I remembered from my youth. I got out at a little café and inquired about the Club Caborrojeño. The man was old enough to know, and he was sober, unlike the stoned, glassy-eyed youth sitting on the bench. He told me that the Club Caborrojeño was on the other side, beyond the town, closer to the area of Guaynabo where I live. I returned to my car, Ilca assuring me that the trip was necessary to better know the place where we had lived for more than a year and a half. But my reason for it had to do with memory. In Guaynabo, the rural is always near; the slick, suburban, middle-class Lexus suddenly runs into Barrio Camarones.

My intuition was correct: the Club Caborrojeño sat very near the Martínez Nadal Expressway, cast away on the lip of modernity, though it is near Guaynabo's Bellas Artes Center. The Club has been abandoned, its shining edifice unkempt, paint peeling away. The grounds are in a state somewhere between neglect and sporadic care. Melancholy hovers in the air, the despair of a place that played host to countless parties and is now silent. I approach the man in charge of the property and ask about Juan Antonio Corretjer's house. "The house isn't there anymore," he says with bitterness and irritation. "It was there, where those pipes are . . ." Ilca drives the car through an entrance adjacent to the Caborrojeño, and we find ourselves in a stand of undergrowth. Piles of black pipe cover much of the site. One can hear the incessant buzzing of the nearby Martínez Nadal Expressway. An abandoned and partially destroyed warehouse, its sign for "Met Imports" peeling away, adds to the desolation and ugliness of the place. Nothing remains of the little woods where I met that poet almost forty years ago. If the Caborrojeño, with its sculpture of the revolutionary Betances, has become such a melancholic place, like the Hotel Casino de la Selva when I visited it on my literary pilgrimage to Cuernavaca in search of scenes from Lowry's *Under the Volcano,* then Corretjer's memory obliges us to despair. Because the house of the poet is sacred ground, only there does the bewildered voice remain, sheltering the tribe.

In that house in the forest, I listened to the poet's wisdom, his apocalyptic vision, and many anecdotes about Albizu Campos and nationalism. Some of the stories were humorous, like the one about October 30, 1950, during the height of the Nationalist revolt, when he went to the store on the Guaynabo town square to buy milk, and how he walked up and down the plaza carrying the two jugs of milk so that no one would think he was involved in the conspiracy. To me, it seemed like something out of a Western, or something anticipating García Márquez's *Chronicle of a Death Foretold.* There, surprised many times by my adolescent rashness, his Mephisthophelean eyebrows would arch emphatically. On his terrace, I spoke with him about how food stamps were a deathblow to independence. When I said this, Corretjer arched his eyebrows even more. I remember when we received Carmín Pérez the week after she was released from prison. That rainy night Corretjer's wife, Doña Consuelo Lee, prepared a Cuban style *mofongo,* a "fufú," which Carmín ate cautiously, not yet used to life outside the prison walls.

I'd forgotten that the entrance was right next to the Caborrojeño, and on the left, because now I'm not sure, but I think I must have come from Río Piedras along what was then called Avenida Central and then turned left to take the old highway—you couldn't miss it because the undercover cops would always be watching across the street from the entrance. That last part, I'm not so sure about; it all seems somewhat illusory to me, like a map stolen from a dream.

2

Avenida del Progreso, My Champs Elysées

I can't remember my first visit to San Juan. Memories, now, are evoked by photographs but even those fade or are lost with each successive move. I suppose that we drove to the sea in the Dodge with whitewall tires because, in one photograph, the car appears together with my elderly grandfather in front of the capitol. It was probably the first time I'd seen the ocean. I don't have the photo at hand, but I remember two distinct versions: in one I have climbed on top of the hood of the Dodge, my grandfather standing beside me, watching in case I fall. He is dressed in long sleeves, suspenders and a tie. A variation of this photo appears in *Puertorriqueños,* only there it is my older brother who watches over me dressed in pants too short for his age.

The other photo is more formal and possibly a dream: I am there with the same short pants and white shirt; my grandfather is at my side dressed in his finest white linen, a man from another age. The jacket appears too small for him. He is an apparition in white a few years before his death.

Directly behind us, facing the Atlantic, stands the Capitol, designed by Rafael Carmoega, evoking an aristocratic world echoed in the face of my grandfather. In front of us lies the blinding light, the dense, salty marine air, and the freedom I felt for the first time, the same freedom to which my grandfather was now saying goodbye. In one of the pictures my eyes are partly closed, punished by the glare. We are dressed in white, reflecting the brilliance we yearned for, a brilliance later lost.

The next picture was taken in 1957 when we moved to the Alamein development on the Avenida 65 de Infantería. World War II and the Korean War were still a part of recent memory resulting in a rash of military place-names. The shadow of dishonor that had fallen over the 65th Infantry in Korea having long been forgotten, we insisted on seeing, in the wasteland where the housing development was built, the desert where Montgomery routed Rommel. My parents and my uncle appear in the picture. We are gathered on the balcony, and I'm sitting at the edge of a planter. It's a special occasion, perhaps a Sunday lunch, because I'm wearing my favorite shirt. Whoever snapped the photo took it from the front lawn and must have been standing less than fifteen feet from the avenue, close enough to be swept away by the torrent of progress, the implacable traffic. Of course, my father had prevailed in buying the house, but not before giving in to my mother's request for an inclined roof. And who took that picture? The knowledge is hidden in memory. If the photographer's identity were the subject of a detective novel, the clues would be elliptical, leading us back to the scene of the crime. Everyone except my brother is in the picture. But it's impossible he took it, as he was studying in Mayagüez at the time. At that age, we all become somewhat allergic to our families, of that I'm sure. And what of the neighbor? Unlikely. We had just moved there and barely knew him.

In *Puertorriqueños,* I said that at nighttime we played ball in the avenue, cars rarely passing by. The avenues were constructed in the fifties as a solution to the increase in cars brought by the burgeoning idea of Progress. Today the avenues are designed as a reaction, a quick fix to the traffic jams. Back then the highway planners were prospective, now they are corrective. My father didn't realize that the car would travel faster than the dream of his utopian frontage road and that the recently named Área Metropolitana would be a cancer, not a blessing.

But, coming from a small town, I had to make the city mine, put some order to my new surroundings. You could say that I had some understanding of city life. But in reality it was not true. Back then what I'm about to describe felt strange to me, even disturbing. Only now do I understand the city as a type of psychic adventure, or perhaps an adventure of the soul, a place where I could lose my balance, allow myself to fall. However, my innocence and fear got in the way, the fear of my own mental fragility, a fragility that never really existed. The new city was like a skein of my fears culminating in my insatiable curiosity. It's fitting, now, that my imagined city transcends time. I narrate the story from the graffiti on the walls. At eleven years old, after the move, life was only about contemplating that unfamiliar wall, feeling trapped by the idea of Progress, the highway lying fifteen feet away, that suicide each family carries with them when they move, bound up in that resplendent and unyielding wall of alienation.

The sensation was exactly like losing one's center, like having saved the furniture but thrown away the house. I no longer had the plaza beneath my balcony. To reconstruct a place, to give it a certain sentimental order, familiarity, and, at the same time make it neurotically memorable, would lead to humiliation. Faced with disorder, I yearned for my grandmother's fields while my bucolic spirit learned the criminal instincts of the streets.

It was a question of training myself. If I walked a straight line out to the sidewalk a few feet away, I would be run down by the torrent of traffic. I clung to the bushes; it was my first humiliation. My first suburban sensation was that I couldn't cross the street in a straight line from my house. As I was very shy about riding the bus, inhaling the smells of rural people, my only option was to walk the avenue dressed in the Khaki military uniform of the San José Preparatory School. At eleven years old, everything, for me, was inordinately difficult. I had to skirt around the avenue to the east and to the west. For the first time, I understood that life for the city pedestrian was, even in the fifties, a series of prohibitions, or, at least, restrictions. In fact, it was my neurotic shyness that made me a pedestrian in the first place. It poured rain so hard the first day I walked to the San José Preparatory School along the 65 de Infantería that the red lining of my backpack ran. I arrived at my house soaking wet and also, it seemed, bleeding. My menopausal mother screamed. Our nerves were on end those first days on the avenue. I spent a long time trying to convince her that I hadn't been hit by a car or attacked by "The Commandos," a group of men who went around slicing women's butts in 1957.

Zooming automobiles and getting into and out of the *marquesinas* or garages that accessed the avenue marked the tempo of the time. The *marquesinas* were the latest thing in Puerto Rican urban architecture, designed as a cover against the rain and as access to the home for a modern, motorized humanity. Drivers flew in and out of them wildly, as if putting on a show. "Dangerous," my father would say because you had to take a sharp turn at high speed to avoid the honking cars and keep up with the speeding traffic. The pedestrian was the first victim. I felt besieged by the steel made in Detroit. The sidewalks bordering the avenue carried out their symbolic function as reminders of a city that had grown beyond its limits. When I was eleven, the ironing ladies—one of whom worked for us—were the only ones beside myself to risk crossing the sidewalks accessing these *marquesinas* in order to go from east to west. We should have had rearview mirrors like the cars. There is nothing like the neurosis that comes from one fear piled upon the other: it was the sensation, while facing traffic that each day became more deafening and crazed, of always having a blind spot, of having to guess which car might jump the sidewalk to avoid a collision, knocking you into the air, or which car might suddenly turn into one of the damned *marquesinas*.

In the twenties, my absent-minded, architect grandfather designed a house that was never built. The plans detailed a *marquesina* with a high ceiling, the height of a train platform. And I ask myself now if his being one of the first car owners in the town, if that architectural distortion somehow transformed that garage into a prophesy of the modernization to come. Over the *marquesina,* my grandfather designed a terrace that expanded the second story of the house, foretelling what would soon become so much a part of the Puerto Rican foolishness seen in the architecture of Puerto Nuevo, Campo Rico, San Agustín and Caparra Terrace.

The seeds of the "society of consumption" lay dormant. If you took a left and headed west, passing by the Tastee Freez built in 1958—I have yet to recover from the "flavor" of those first Tastee Freez burgers—you would arrive at the strip mall directly in front of the monument to the 65th Infantry. Plunged deep into our pedestrian adventure, we would arrive at new spaces somewhere between that same Tastee Freez and the roadside dives, bars, and restaurants, which the 65 de Infantería should reclaim as its right. Designed for the car and the revelers of the bygone Friday nightlife, these bars became the frontier between lechery and drunkenness for the suburban savages, the beer and rum drinkers who, in the seventies, acquired a taste for Lancers's wine. Lugo's, like the other roadside bars, used Formica to create a modern look. Inside, the cast iron seats didn't encourage the worker from Fuentes Fluviales to pull the chair out for his girl. The immense bar with its high-backed stools seated the occasional whore in the same corner where Papo Newman, Vigoreaux's murderer, once hung out. In that corner of Lugo's, they fostered a crude, suburban style that will be with us forever, a style that Gabriel Suau, together with the "Gangster," adapted for television. And there, in front, like a hallucination at eight in the evening, the neon sign hung, bigger than any I'd seen in recent years, its message written in enormous letters: *TODOS.*

The strip mall's parking lot is next to Lugo's. It appears in all the *libros de oro* of the time—annual books published as a vain symbol of our development, an emblem of the new, vigorous, and invincible Puerto Rico. In the earliest pictures taken of the parking lot and the avenue, there weren't many cars; Bel Airs appeared in 1956 and Impalas in the early sixties. The Lugo's sign later changed to a sign for the Grand Union and now the Grande supermarket. All, in the end, would lose their drawing power. We grew accustomed to watching the local ma and pa shop turn into a supermarket and the roadside bar, with its turbid hungers, become an avenue bar servicing the motels that rise unabated. With muddied shoes we pressed on, entering the first frenzied Los Angeles–style suburbs. The city grew toward the benign pole of the new middle class, leaving crime and drugs in its wake. We passed gangs hanging out on the corner, trying to score a hit.

However, in 1957 we were still far from the worst effects of suburbia. On Río Piedras hill—besieged by the 65 de Infantería, which once stood between Capetillo and Buen Consejo—there stood yet another site from my troubled eleventh year: the San José Preparatory School whose neon sign illuminated that corner of the 65th Infantry with a splendor from another world, yet another vain symbol of modern times. I spent three years of my childhood and four of my adolescence there. Just above the beginning of the 65 de Infantería, next to the Buen Consejo neighborhood, it was a place of solace, a gift to a life altered by rabid Progress and the quiet expectations of a family move.

The profile of the San José Preparatory School towered above the monument to the 65th Infantry Regiment, its majesty undiminished by the idea of Progress represented in that profane highway. It was founded in the thirties as a boys' school called San Agustín; later, in the forties, it was run by the Marianist order. The school stood diagonally across from the monument, its new wing built in the mid-fifties and overlooking the avenue in order to accommodate the new road that would border Río Piedras. A landmark, the school dignified the new urban landscape.

More than a school, the place seemed to have emerged from the mind of my absent-minded grandfather; it was *criollo* in its ambition. Climbing from Calle Los Marianistas in Río Piedras, a hike I had to make every day, the steep slope ended at the entrance designed in the

Californian "Spanish Revival" architecture of the thirties. The so-called *marquesina* stood out prominently and resembled the plan my grandfather used for his new house, except with art-deco moldings for the eaves. The high ceiling and width of the platform were designed so that the wealthy parents of the forties could drop off their children each morning without leaving their car. The cement benches donated by the prominent families of San Juan with their fancy-sounding names caught my attention from the first day of school. A California-style church tower with a roof and cornice made of tile and a metal cross at its apex culminated the view up the hill.

Looking to the left from the roof of the *marquesina,* the entire silhouette of Río Piedras to Hato Rey can be seen below, a sprawling expanse of streets marked by one- and two-story structures reminiscent of Puerto Rico in the thirties and forties, the urban landscape of the Antilles brushed with occasional yet exuberant greenery, and to the far left, the University Tower, an image of a Caribbean population on the margins of American style progress. In Fort de France, many years later, I would see the same landscape aglow with light, with tin roofs and wraparound balconies. From the cement cross of the San José Preparatory School, positioned just in front of the *marquesina,* I was able to look out over Río Piedras and see the mist rising off the bay and San Juan beyond. To glimpse what was beginning to be called the Área Metropolitana was, for me at eleven years old, an initiation into a type of meditation, into the certainty that the city below was also an extension of my life.

In front of me is the cloister, that interior patio I described in *Sol de medianoche,* the dream space that became a nightmare for the antihero, Manolo. In the novel, the school on the hill is located on the Vigía de Ponce, with the Caribbean in the distance. The architect Rafael Carmoega visited the school in 1957 in order to supervise the installation of an enormous statue, *San José obrero* (Saint Joseph, the worker), in front of the main entrance to the balcony. The architect was tall and, like my grandfather, exhibited a patrician baldness. The building itself required work: the beautifully designed Spanish

Revival of the old structure at the top of the hill had to blend in with the wing constructed in the early fifties that looks out over the modern Avenida 65 de Infantería.

It was called the *colegio de blanquitos,* the "school for little, rich white kids." Looking out over the scenic street that ran in front of the *marquesina,* a street shielded by rows of palm trees, fronds blowing in the wind, I discovered my own privileged place, one that inspired in me a neurotic introspection, which either leads to the monastery or the university. It was that simple. During the day, the school was little more than a reformatory for rich kids, but after two thirty I contemplated the city from on high, called by the enigma of its streets. My curiosity was a caress fitting to my age, passing through my groin before reaching my mind.

My first streets were those of Río Piedras, especially the long one that ran from the Avenida Ponce de León to the Sabana Llana sector. It is the axis that connects the rural people—the people who frequent the popular markets and street vendors—to semi-rural suburbia.

These people came from the opposite pole to my latitude on the 65 de Infantería. That is to say, if I left my house and walked the thirteen steps to the sidewalk, the precipice before the torrent of progress, and turned right, going east toward the semi-rural neighborhoods, I would have ended my short jaunt in what is today the crossroad of Trujillo Alto, the entryway to el Vate's *bohío,* where twenty-something years later I would meet with the man responsible for so many moves. *Las tribulaciones de Jonás* were always near the scene of the crime.

Before they built the Concordia condominium complex, the corner was working class, similar in spirit to the Bulón neighborhood. If we went north, along the roadway intersected by the 65 de Infantería, we would arrive in Sabana Llana and the east end of Calle de Diego. There they talked, shot billiards, and ate fried *alcapurrias* and tripe, at least until Tastee Freez took over. On that corner, street vendors hawked everything from cheap jewelry to the latest transistor radios and much-desired joints. However, it was not the place to score a hit. It was really more of an excuse for men to get together and joke around than it was a corner for drug deals—something like a town gathering at the local pharmacy.

The 65 de Infantería had one foot in the rural, in a space somewhere between the city and the country. It was a place where my father's frontage road would never appear, a place cast aside, rendered invisible by Progress. Farther to the east, toward Carolina, stood the Comandante Racetrack, built in the late fifties. My childhood was marked by baseball, my adolescence by horses. I oscillated between sonorous surnames, two-syllable nicknames, such as Guille, Tito, and Cuqui, and the names of those who cared for horses, names like Falú, Paniagua, and Pillot.

On the corner sat the Pastrana family bar, made famous throughout Avenida 65 de Infantería and Río Piedras by its cutting-edge architecture. These types of bars were characterized by the fact that they clung to the side of the highway, cars speeding by just beyond the glass doors, portals to the melancholy night. Inside, the stench of gin and cigarettes, and still more the faint blue and whorish light illuminating the darkness, numbing the mind. The fancy Formica, along with the high-backed bar stools and cast iron chairs defined the place. In a fight, you couldn't throw the furniture. I suppose it was places like these that invented fried chicken cracklings to cure the effects of the fragrant Superior Rum. It was also these places where I'd go to smoke and drink, to do anything that would make me different from my father. There, too, I discovered sex and the irony of women.

On this corner of 65 de Infantería and the road to Trujillo Alto there was a small strip mall. During the height of their fame, the Pastrana family built their newest bar, Don's, at the intersection of Calle de Diego and the so-called Carpenter Road. The old Don's stood where the 65 de Infantería began, in the lower levels of a building that today houses the Hotel Roxy. Behind the new Don's stood another working-class bar with the evocative name of Capri, referring not to the island of Capri where the Roman Emperor Tiberius kept his palace, but rather to the nearby suburb, Villa Capri. There, the

sarcasm of the woman behind the bar generally killed off the flip-
pant street talk. She used to serve me gin with Coco Rico.

In all of Puerto Rican painting and photography, I know of only
one painting that depicts this new urban landscape of avenues and
viaducts conquered by the automobile. It is one of José Ruiz's mini-
atures painted in the early seventies: in the distance, we see the neon
signs and lights of the city, closer in the lampposts, their long arms
outstretched like gulls' wings, the latest invention to illuminate the
streets and avenues of the post-fifties world. An elevated viaduct rising above a grassy and treeless field stretches out before us. The focus
of the painting is on this viaduct where we see endless taillights. The
viaduct stands imposingly on four enormous pillars. Still more gull-
like light posts crest the viaduct lending an atmosphere of twilight
serenity. We know this because the indigo-blue sky remains pale
while the horizon below grows dark.

However, it is in the foreground that we recognize the Pastrana
family's architecture, a two-story masterwork. On the second floor,
under a parapet without eaves and decorated by dismal corner-
pieces, large windows are cranked open. They are a variation on the
so-called Miami windows. In the front of the building, just above
the semi-circle eaves so popular in that decade, hangs a surreal sign
announcing "Copas," a word rarely used in Puerto Rico; it's as if it
were a lexical invention of José Ruiz. Beside it, there is a neon goblet
vaguely resembling a daiquiri or, perhaps, a champagne glass, the
kind used in weddings along Avenida Campo Rico. The magical realism of the orange slice adorning the rim of the glass is a monstros-
ity of the surreal out of proportion with the rest.

Another large window opens over a second eave. With time, it
will collect all the filth from the roof, the street, the viaduct, and the
window above, even the debris left by construction. Lights hang
from the eave, and as we snoop around, we peek into the bar. No
one is there. Bottles line the wall behind the bar, and the stools, this
time without seatbacks, are redolent of diners from the previous
decade. We glimpse a resplendence, as if a ray of light shone from

behind the bar. We wonder if the place has been broken into. There is a car parked on the side of the building, which from its taillights resembles an Impala from the early sixties. The street in front of the bar is like a frontage road to the viaduct; we don't know if the bar has been abandoned, cornered by the viaduct passing over it.

Another car, like a limousine stretched beyond all proportion, moves along the street in front of the bar. The back of the car resembles a Thunderbird from the years when they used too much chrome. Two people sit inside the car, but we don't know if they are casing the place or simply passing by. On the corner in front of the bar, where the sidewalk narrows to almost nothing so that the street practically runs into the bar entrance, we see a solitary lamppost, illuminated. Its isolation adds to the sadness of the scene. José Ruiz seems to be telling us that people rarely pass there on the sidewalk. A pearly light emanates from the neon sign. The gray light fades as we reach the tall grass growing under the viaduct. They cut the grass recently and left it piled there. It has since turned brown as no one has come to bag it. We don't know if the scene is one of abandonment, desolation, or imminent violence, but it holds a loneliness that reminds us of Hopper's "Nighthawks," painted in 1942.

Mostly, though, the scene is reminiscent of the corner near the Capri bar. When the Trujillo Alto Expressway was unveiled with great fanfare, the bar I frequented in my adolescence still remained there on the outskirts, inconvenient and already nearly forgotten, tending toward the melancholic in the knowledge of having been left behind.

I don't know why I identify César Andreu Iglesias's novel *The Vanquished* with that type of bar. But I remember that I had my first barroom affair while I was reading the novel. Her name was Epi, and she worked behind the counter. The novel obviously unleashed the quixotic in me. I left defending her for all to see; I don't know why I did it. Perhaps the mixture of her womanly scent with literature and my own adolescent loneliness intoxicated me.

3

A Long and Caribbean Street

While the commercial center on Avenida 65 de Infantería celebrated the opening of one of the first bowling alleys in San Juan, I walked along the edge of Progress, the mile between the San José Preparatory School and my house. The frontage road we'd yearned for never arrived; my father's absurd purchase, made on the shore of that deafening traffic, was never vindicated. Had there been a street running parallel to the avenue, it too would have tasted the bitter fruits of marginalization, of not being worthy of the present, yet unable to return to the past, left on the roadside like the bars of the Pastrana family.

I spent much of my youth and a good part of my adulthood on Calle de Diego. Today the sector it runs through, called Sabana Llana, connects with the coast of Isla Verde through the Avenida Iturregui and the Moscoso Bridge. But the first memory that comes to mind goes back to 1968 when I married and moved to a new condominium complex ambitiously named Green Village. Much later, in 1978, I moved to a bigger unit in the same complex, with a view of the city below stretching to the sea, a view similar to the one I'd had from the *marquesina* of the San José Preparatory School. Much of my literary output was written in the study of that home. From there, I could take in the nearby San José Lagoon, the distant shoreline of Isla

Verde, and, in the last years of my time there, the construction of the
Moscoso Bridge. My experience of the urban landscape from the
heights of the tenth floor was different from that of the lower levels,
all traces of the ground erased by the dense, tropical vegetation spill-
ing into the sea. The scene would calm my nerves; it was my way of
taking in the air and the atmosphere of the city, of divining its essence. It was a way of living with the sea before me and the 65 de
Infantería at my back. My life, like the city itself, searched for its
own metaphor.

Beneath the balcony of my study, across the condominium parking lot, on the other side of Calle de Diego, sits El Jibarito Bar and
Grill and the house of the architect Henry Klumb. Both are distinguished by tree-lined pathways, an important part of my recupera-
tion from a childhood that knew the country but had been banished
to the Avenue. El Jibarito sits on the corner between de Diego and
Calle Ramón B. López, which passes in front of the Lopez Sicardo
housing project. But this isn't another roadside bar like those of the
Pastrana family. It boasts an outdoor patio and jukebox. Even with
the volume at full blast, the jukebox can't compete with the cars
zooming by at fifty miles per hour, though it can compete with the
rustling leaves of the tall, yellow oak tree that flowers in May and
whose shade in March and April sways with the changing breeze. It
is where the writer Luis Rafael Sánchez, who also lived in Green Village, would have his picture taken beside the jukebox wearing his
"Truman" shirt with palm trees to drive home his Caribbean identity. It is a place one wouldn't suspect in this urban landscape, a bar
that dreamed, in the best case, of a gathering of writers, just like the
European outdoor cafés, except for the fact that it was frequented by
petty government officials who came for a beer before surrendering
to the despair of fighting the traffic jam on the 65 de Infantería that
stretched to Canóvanas. Having become familiar with this cityscape,
I transformed El Jibarito into Manolo's hang out, his place for a
quick drink and long hangovers in my novel *Mujer con sombrero
Panamá*. In the novel he lived in the building next to El Jibarito with

his dysfunctional family: his longhaired dachshund, Canelo, and the crazy Commander Carabine, son of Ronald Reagan and Lucy Boscana, the Puerto Rican actress.

Behind the gate seen from the terrace of El Jíbarito was hidden the tropical house of the master architect Henry Klumb, who designed many of the modern buildings at the University of Puerto Rico. With a corrugated tin roof and hardly any walls, the house opened to the dense foliage of a tropical grove, adding secrecy to privacy. Surrounded by urban vulgarity, yet at the same time remote from Puerto Rico, the house sat protected in the middle of a small forest, as the eaves protected the veranda from the thundering rain, an appropriate metaphor of exclusivity. The house of this disciple of Frank Lloyd Wright was little more than a shelter built in the middle of the forest, yet it became an emblem for all the stranded gringo houses built in the tropics, like that of William Sinz, a professor of Latin, who sold his house on Trujillo Alto to Muñoz Marín in the second half of the forties, and in whose *bohío,* almost thirty years later, I conceived the idea for the interview with "el Vate" that culminated in *Las tribulaciones de Jonás.* The houses were built in the forest or in a tropical garden, as was the case with el Vate's house, or the house of the Caribbean social historian, Gordon Lewis, who lived in the Trujillo Alto neighborhood oddly named Saint Just. Uninfluenced by Klumb's city garden design, the home of the sculptor, George Warreck, remained stranded in the University of Puerto Rico's faculty residence on the end of old Carpenter Road, a place reserved for the gringos who came during the true colonial era. Between these gringos and the new Puerto Rico, whom they helped to educate, understand, or contradict, lay the verdant jungle, as if the less desirable realization of Progress was reserved only for the colonized. The gringos lived as if in a bubble, trapped in the metaphor of their Caribbean fate. Our Caribbean would be more capricious in its urban eccentricities, with more billboards, more cement, and less romance and scenery.

For example, the well-to-do families in Río Piedras used to live on Calle de Diego in the Sabana Llana sector where Río Piedras exits to Carolina. There we see the scattered ruins of ancestral homes, the tall grass almost covering the terraces, and the gable of the tin, four-sided roof hanging over the balconies. One house is raised on a mound overlooking Calle de Diego. A path leads from the road to the front steps, rising at such a steep incline that it seems it will continue to the gable of the roof. A solitary palm tree besieged by the tall underbrush appears to be an afterthought of the designer, shattering the optical illusion and returning us to the true scale of things. As we descend from Sabana Llana, we note the house on the left and the urban discontinuity forced upon the fifties neighborhood of Río Piedras. It is a ranch house designed in that time period, a house that seems to be in the wrong neighborhood. It should have been built in Garden Hills and not in this place plagued by urban decadence. The enormous, stone façade hides the desolate entrance. The ample front lawn with its distinct levels must have excited the owner so much that he claimed part of the old sidewalk of de Diego. The street was already overlooked in the fifties, so that they must have felt the few pedestrians didn't merit a sidewalk. Isolated more and more from Río Piedras, the Sabana Llana neighborhood became abandoned, its reputation diminished, left to the ambition of the Dominican immigrants. Meanwhile, the automobile ruled the parallel street, Avenida 65 de Infantería, the one beginning at the Hotel Roxy, which was Don's at that time, the confluence between the Calle de Diego of Río Piedras and the one that climbs to the Sabana Llana, the place where Carpenter Road ends and my Champs Elysées begins, the interweaving of an urban tapestry.

Heading toward Carolina and just past the old town route, we recall the sugar cane plantations and cultivated citrus fields, mostly of grapefruit, that lined the road now converted into a thoroughfare. Today all that has disappeared. Only the ancestral memory of the fields remains. Near the end of the sixties, condominiums replaced the land once owned by the middle-class Río Piedras professionals, symbolizing a shift from the suburban house to a vertical lifestyle. Many of us young University of Puerto Rico professors at the Río Piedras campus lived in them. My own time on that street was memorable. Beyond the Pennock Gardens, which I visited with my parents and which bordered a rural area I don't remember, stood the Pastrana's Mango Tree, the definitive roadside restaurant en route to the first red-light motel whose glare would attract a new type of customer in Trujillo Alto. In this later version, however, the Pastranas abandoned the inconvenience of a corner location on the Avenue in favor of a circular dining hall positioned beneath a great mango tree. The thundering rain upon the tin roof created the perfect atmosphere for intimacy. The Pastrana's Mango Tree was a sort of prototype for El Jibarito Bar and Grill, a model that was necessary in order to move from breaded minute steaks with fried plantains to conch salads. According to the *Elogio de la fonda,* the memory of the city is unlocked in the flavors of the food. The Mango Tree was where Manolo had an attack of *vesania,* or rage, on his way to breaking with Commander Carabine. It was the time when, in a crazed state, Manolo humiliated the Commander, throwing fried plantains and pieces of conch in his face. It was the *Wut*—the impulsive act before the loss of courage—that Christopher Isherwood reviews in *Goodbye Berlin.* Returning to his apartment alongside El Jibarito, in the midst of the fog of alcohol and the buzz of marijuana, Manolo was pursued by that word, *vesania,* because his anger had hurt the pride of his Commander, a fury as mysterious as the meaning of that word, forgotten in the depths of the dictionary.

In my novel *Mujer con sombrero Panamá,* I attempted to describe Calle de Diego with its working-class rhythm: the two-story boarding houses available only to single males, built in the forties and fifties by generic architects whose work is defined by its cancerous, gray design; the uncountable auto-repair shops; the vendor halfway between the street market and the grocery store; the pharmacy preferred by thieves; the tire shop and the front-suspension mechanic;

the noisy Dominican neighborhood bustling to the clackity-clack of flip-flops; the eatery where Saturdays the aroma of saucy tripe fills the air; so much street life, like the blue street vendor damned by Hugo who sets up shop at eleven in the morning on Fridays offering fried *bacalaitos* and *alcapurrias*. It is a working-class existence, a breath away from the desperation of the drug addict or the cunning of the dealer. I ask myself if the western world should care about a street like this, one so impossible to describe. I suppose similar places exist in the working-class neighborhoods on the outskirts of Paris. The attempt to recreate it in literature with the idea that some reader in Madrid might actually see and feel the place is, perhaps, crazy and pretentious. To think that the electric cables running along the posts and crossbeams of Calle de Diego merit attention is neurotic at best.

It would be easier to describe, with a few historical and sociological allusions, how at the western end of Calle de Diego, past the Hotel Roxy until you hit Río Piedras, the human landscape turns rural. Here is where Calle de Diego, along with Calle Loíza, is the symbol of our Caribbean identity, located within that crowd of shoppers who can't decide between the street market and the food vendor, between the rural and the urban. It is only when Calle de Diego hits Ponce de Léon that it becomes a major thoroughfare full of urban pretension and a sophisticated past. However, my street remains indescribable. Perhaps, for that reason, it is easier to see it from on high, to capture it with a glance. It would appear in the foreground as something benign rising from the labyrinth of streets and plush backyards that stretch to the misty coast of the Atlantic beyond.

Lending dignity to the scene, a dubious task, I would say that in these modest dwellings, on this very street, Mario Vargas Llosa wrote *Conversación en La Catedral,* Luis Rafael Sánchez perhaps conceived and wrote much of *La guaracha del Macho Camacho,* and a young dreamer completed *La noche oscura del Niño Avilés.* For a time, Vargas Llosa lived in the Windsor Towers Condominiums and Sánchez in Green Village. Amaury Veray, the author of the beloved song

"Villancico Yaucano," lived in the De Diego condominium complex and, in later years, sought succor from his Puerto Rican sorrows by praying the rosary and drinking Coors in the little Piñero Plaza with the neighborhood drunks, who, by the glassy look in their eyes at eleven in the morning, had already downed a few cold ones.

4

In Search of the City of Letters

On the street paralleling the wall of the San José Preparatory School and set atop a hill, apart from the other streets in Río Piedras, stood a house that evoked my adolescent desires. It was on the corner of Padres Capuchinos, at the end of Calle La Paz where it runs into the San Antonio School. I converted the two-story building with its tin roof and dilapidated balcony into a place for my literary fantasies. In *La chambre claire,* Roland Barthes said that the photographs of some houses of the urban landscape are not only "visitable" but also "livable." Barthes goes on to discuss a house photographed by Charles Clifford around 1854: "This longing to inhabit, if I observe it clearly in myself, is neither oneiric (I do not dream of some extravagant site) nor empirical (I do not intend to buy a house according to the views of a real-estate agency); it is fantasmatic, deriving from a kind of second sight which seems to bear me forward to a utopian time, or to carry me back to somewhere in myself: a double movement which Baudelaire celebrated in 'Invitation au voyage' and 'La vie antérieure.'"

It was that double movement of longing that I felt in front of that house. I continued looking at that house even after class was over. I was sixteen or seventeen, and it was easy to discern that three-in-the-afternoon light, a light I yearned for, and for which I would continue to search throughout the imagined city, a light that signified for me a delicate bond with the home we left behind in Aguas Buenas. The house tempted me because I'd lived in a similar one with split-levels and balconies that marked the sun's passage into twilight. I imagined myself living in that house, the doors opening to the creamy afternoon light. It was the "solar" aspect of my desire.

But the "lunar" side of that spectral yearning also manifested itself in this house of forbidden dreams. Back then I was reading the 1958 New Directions edition of *The Flowers of Evil,* which I bought in the Minerva bookstore near bus stop 15 ½. "Invitation au voyage" was my favorite poem with its adolescent longing for distant lands and artificial paradise of sex and tobacco. For at that time, I imagined the house with its doors closed, a pipe on a table alongside the divan and the voluptuous figure of the "negress" in the shadows: *luxe, calme et volupté,* all Baudelaire's relatives, whom my family would never invite for Thanksgiving turkey.

It was the double fantasy of denying the progress of the 65 de Infantería and longing for the streets, for the Baudelairian multitudes, with the *flâneur's* gaze as the method of knowledge. The effect was that my interior life existed elsewhere. I was a neurotic adolescent, walking forgotten streets, my gaze lowered, peering into little-known alleyways, memorizing the dates stamped on sewer drains, studying the cracks in the streets and sidewalks. My obsession was to look within; the tobacco-induced coma was transformed into desire. I think, now, that it must have been a remnant of uterine yearning, whether hysteric or historic, a search for the origin, for the veiled frontier that is sex.

The crazed impulse toward that house was not a great method for arriving at knowledge. I realized it soon enough. It was like running aground in ridiculous self-absorption. It was necessary, in the Joycean manner—because Joyce was the other literary idol of my youth—to open to the sound of the city, to listen to its voices, to eavesdrop on its speech at the bus stop, at the vendor's stands on Calle de Diego, in the little bars in Capetillo or the ones along the roadside of the 65 de Infantería. Because that other condition of my soul was like living in a silent movie, in a languid, symbolist, or expressionist space, according to the mood of the day, a consolation for my pimples, hand jobs, and expensive cigarettes. But, of what importance is desire? I was not a son of Paris or of Dublin. Laguerre's novels bored me. I preferred those of César Andreu Iglesias. Nothing of the tragic countryside for me! The object of my consciousness was marked as much by desire as by self-denial. In other words, I was ready to enter the University of Puerto Rico.

I understood intuitively that the city of letters existed in the opposite direction from Avenida 65 de Infantería. It was necessary to walk to downtown Río Piedras, arriving by late afternoon at the acoustic shell of Convalescencia Plaza, a place of past nobility and present poverty, a place resounding with the poetic verse of Gregory Corso, Lawrence Ferlinghetti, Allen Ginsberg, and the impetuous novels of Jack Kerouac. The beat poets, with their spontaneity and aloof vision of sordid city life, were the necessary guides in my confrontation with the marginalized and dispossessed urban landscape of Río Piedras. I was not merely content to eat ice cream at the recently established Los Chinitos, or to listen repeatedly to the oration of a fellow student—the Cuban, Raimundo Travieso—regarding how fruit sorbet was invented in Havana.

Those twilight sojourns along Avenida Ponce de León, darkness falling like a premonition of a life gone wrong, inspired my first poem. Lazy as usual, I wrote it in prose, in the manner of Baudelaire, arising more out of disgust than craft. I don't know if it gave, then, a sign of my future ambition. It was titled "The Last Samurai" and was a sort of guesswork into the lives of the poor and dispossessed in Río Piedras. Today I would say the samurai was a homeless man who didn't pay his social security, but back then that samurai was a Joycean epiphany, the revelation of an urgent feeling that my memory has now lost. I suppose it was a poem about a person who took a wrong turn in life. The samurai was at war with the sadness of the streets and the finality of the mistakes that hurled us into them. I used to frequent the art cinema at the University of Puerto Rico, and during my walks, head lowered beneath darkening skies, through streets with gutters overflowing, I conceived of that poem inspired by Kurosawa's epic. I was sixteen years old and a suburban romantic.

I was on the road of Ponce de León, which was like the road to the University of Puerto Rico, characterized by my crazy ambition for intellectual life. The large, two-story houses, built at the beginning of the twentieth century, had, by the sixties, already seen their best days and now served as homes for the middle class. Now, they're gone, but not without a trace. The ruins of these once noble houses formed part of my melancholy. Only the cynical commentaries made by the young hoodlums at the big screen of the Paradise Theater in Río Piedras could free me from my self-absorption. I walked the streets with the pride of one who has no fear, the catatonia of longing feeding my alienation.

I was a son of urban disorder, of the dispossessed and the marginalized, of an urbanized and declassed middle class, a frequenter of roadside bars and the sarcasm of whores disguised as waitresses. I was a son of a Champs Elysées that would have frightened Baudelaire himself. Because of this, it was necessary that I turn right on Ponce de León and pass with trepidation the Paradise Theater and La Torre Bar and Restaurant to get to the real tower, the one of ivory, the symbol of the University of Puerto Rico in the style of its rector, Jaime Benítez. For my lost innocence, I found a deceptive and comic place where I remained for thirty-two years. Pedantry is the best remedy for suburban romanticism. Yet, as I arrived at the gates and faced the Tower, prepared to cross over, to enter the avenue of palm trees, I felt as if I'd been transported to a magic place, a utopia, a forgotten land of childhood dreams. In the manner of Stephen Daedalus, I held high the chalice of pretension. It was an initiation into a city of letters within a city of ignorance.

My mother was a fan of the university rector, Jaime Benítez, who presided over the graduation ceremonies of the fifties and sixties. His golden oratory and extravagant gestures consoled my menopausal mother, who urged me to watch the ceremonies on television, not realizing that within her son grew an interest for a vocation far from the ambitions of the middle class in their ranch houses. To become a professor was to undermine an intellect that should have been used to become a doctor, a lawyer, or possibly an engineer. I told her that only people with a talent for math would make the best salaries.

To arrive at the University of Puerto Rico, through a Río Piedras that, though it still managed to glimmer, was beginning to decay, was, for me, to stumble into the alternate, interior space of the intellect, into a type of "garden city" university. Jaime Benítez's university was a risky proposition in the land of the mambo and the cha-cha.

In *Los cuentos de la Universidad,* Emilio S. Belaval tells us of a university defined by the privileges of class, of young gentlemen in coats and ties, with mustaches reminiscent of Clark Gable. Opposite of working men, they were candidates for the upper class in the Ortegan sense. In the most superficial version, they would be the *petit maître* or "el flan" (a variant of *flanêur*) impressed by their own membership in Phi Sigma or Phi Eta. When I arrived at the University of Puerto Rico, some of these gentlemen had continued on as professors. Their conduct and manner of dress offered me an alternative model of Puerto Rican male behavior. Even though some were great dancers, like those at Phi Eta, they now exhibited the monastic sadness characteristic of their introspective life, an unusual thing in these *machista* lands.

In 1964 the University of Puerto Rico was on its way to a better democracy. That year would see the revival of the student movement and the first riots since 1948. The pompous rector of the university would test his valor when he was confronted by an angry mob of students near the university's south gate. We were moving from the Spanish Revival or Spanish Renaissance architecture, conceived by the vanguard in the twenties and thirties, to the level and expansive tropical architecture of Henry Klumb. If the University Tower marked a hierarchy of superior intellectual nobility and purpose, sprinkled with tiles and Moorish ornaments for exotic effect, Henry

Klumb would propose a functional architecture with cross ventilation more focused on the tropical surroundings than on any attempt to serve as a symbol of privilege. Like the San José Preparatory School with its California-style tower, the University of Puerto Rico saw rapid change during those years. Rafael Carmoega adapted his style to the new times, but the task fell to Henry Klumb to fix Carmoega's vision of the university's central quadrangle. The school atop the mountain of Buen Consejo opened a conduit to the intellectual garden of the university. For me, it was a type of autobiographical pilgrimage. The cloisters—their archways like Caribbean galleries, their tile roofs and Greek columns reminding us of the stuffy dignity of scholarly pursuits—connected the offices, hallways, and classrooms. Under tropical rains, the university became more intimate, the hallways more conducive to intellectual gatherings of the elite than to angry student rallies.

The university of the twenties, thirties, and forties, with its Moorish appearance and monastic cloisters so distant from the urban fabric of Río Piedras, was transforming itself into an alternative space for a culture that was feeling the assault of Americanization. At the same time, there were rumors that the university, with its *petit maîtres,* also sheltered conservative Hispanophiles and neofascists. Stories circulated, some comic, such as the one propagated by Hugh Thomas in the first edition of *The Spanish Civil War:* the judge, Enjuto, who condemned José Antonio Primo de Rivera to prison, was thrown from University Tower by a group of Falangist students, a distortion of a Hispanophile legend that converted the father of Jorge Enjuto into a Caribbean Cola di Rienzo.

In 1964 the prairie style turned ranch house had already been adapted to the educational needs of the tropics, which were beginning to be codified by Henry Klumb. The alternative space represented by the University of Puerto Rico was no longer aristocratic and Hispanophile, but populist, owing more of a debt to Frank Lloyd Wright than to the Alhambra. The buildings would offer ample entryways for protection from the torrential tropical rains, as well as for listening to the fiery words of *Fidelismo.* The lobby of the Social Sciences Building would provide the perfect place for invoking the name of Ché Guevara. Marches and protests would be substituted for fraternity initiations as rites of adolescent passage inspired by the anxiety of belonging. The so-called student center with its populist meeting hall and self-service cafeteria would displace the gazebo and picnic grounds. The intellectual city would also suffer the anxieties of the modern era. But, for my nerves fried by the noise of the 65 de Infantería, the university was a sanctuary, a noble home with the attraction of an interior life and the promise of a certain sensuality. What did it matter that the professors who taught *The Iliad* didn't know Greek, or that those who smothered me with Faust didn't know German? We dreamed with a translated European mentality. It was a step out of the peasant culture I had known as a child, the only sure road to overcoming the music of Felipe and Tito Rodríguez.

When I arrived at the university, what stood out most was that it was still inhabited by the ghosts of the city of letters. Pedro Salinas scanned *El Contemplado*'s verses while passing through the university's hallways dressed to the hilt in a white cotton suit and Panama hat. Juan Ramón Jiménez had left a wake of amusing anecdotes told in the mood of a cranky old man. More important, still, was the painter, Eugenio Fernández Granell, who had disembarked in Santo Domingo with Saul Steinberg, André Breton, and other surrealists in flight from Fascism, and who found in the "tristes tropiques" a space for his work on the upper level of the Pintadera Art Shop, facing the Auxilio Mutuo Hospital. It was there he created *El Mirador Azul,* "The Blue Tower," the place of initiation for one of the university's truly original spirits, Roberto "El Boquio" Alberty.

When I entered the University of Puerto Rico in 1964, the last vestiges of what was known as the "blue culture" still remained. I suppose that it came into being in the thirties and forties. As always, it would be a way of positioning ourselves against our vanishing West Indian and Caribbean identity. The "blue culture" was aristocratic and Eurocentric, and, for me, it represented the other side of the self-denial always lurking in the colonial world. Roberto "El Boquio" Alberty learned surrealism from Fernández Granell, but he would have to dream it walking the streets of Río Piedras. The Baudelarian *flâneur* would not metamorphose into "flan" as the younger gentlemen had done, nor would he have the view of the boulevards from the open-air cafés. His imagination sparked by Fernández Granell, El Boquio studied under the G.I. Bill after going to Korea. The rest of El Boquio's life would be tied to the university obliquely, his poetry and art a testament to how Avenida Ponce de Léon imagined itself as another left bank of the Seine. And just as happened in nineteenth-century Paris, the illusory bohemian neighborhood would inevitably be dominated by official buildings, symbolic markers by which the bohemian *flâneur* would recognize his own marginalization.

The university quadrangle would be the symbol of that dream denied by Río Piedras. Designed as an alternative space, it became a fortress, a diminution of everything outside the university cloisters, a synecdoche for everything aspired to within. The addition of the quadrangle to Carmoega's Tower both complemented and contrasted with Convalescencia Plaza in Río Piedras.

In contrast to the university, Río Piedras had its own symbols of ceremony, characterized most notably by three buildings along Avenida Ponce de León. The Church of Pilar in Convalescencia Plaza called to mind, with its two bells reminiscent of the classical age, a spiritual life mediated by the sensuality of the tropics. The ample space of the atrium provided a gathering place that nourished the interior life and, at the same time, a space that welcomed the bustling commercial world outside. The atrium was a symbol that both affirmed and belied its own truths.

The University Tower and quadrangle seem hidden and closed when compared to the Church of Pilar. The church's counterpart was the secular monastery of the university. The quadrangle is exclusive because the interior life that sustains it is intellectual, not spiritual, and still less Catholic. It is a cloister for academic ceremonies whose elitist ambitions would be realized in the graduations held in the University Theater in the front of the quadrangle.

A little more to the north along Ponce de León, we find another ceremonial building: the Auxilio Mutuo Hospital, where the body is healed and the dying eased along their way. It appears almost as an afterthought along the Avenue. Cavafis, the poet of Alexandria, once said that the church, the whorehouse, and the hospital existed together on his street in order to heal all the existential maladies. In Río Piedras, the brothels are near the Parish of Pilar, while the Auxilio Mutuo Hospital stands near that quadrangle, the University Square where we would dream of Europe and cure ourselves of the Caribbean.

Together with the Tower, Carmoega's quadrangle makes an interior garden. With the passing of time, the cloisters would be overrun by lush tropical vegetation, laurels, and Brazilian palms. The rigor of the cloisters would be assuaged, the university would return to the intimacy at its heart. It was a place made for meditation and the contemplation of time. But in fact, the so-called professional students remained in the university for decades. They were street *flâneurs,* like El Boquio, who became aimless wanderers. Cross-eyed Milton and Pepe Down would prefer that place to any other. Though the plaza tried to hide its academic role, almost to the point of erasing the façades of the registrar's office and the University Theater, its function as an interior space dedicated to leisure and contemplative solitude defined its true ambition. At any rate, I would always imagine the quadrangle as another planet in respect to Calle de Diego. It was as if there were two Río Piedras, the quadrangle hidden away, a place that would always remain secret, and de Diego, the Caribbean Río Piedras full of street life. El Boquio crossed the university quadrangle and the marginalized Río Piedras street life caused a shudder in those monastic cloisters.

The city of letters needs privileged corners, like that of La Torre Restaurant and Bar, where the streets of Río Piedras get nervous looking at the symbol of the *Cité Universitaire.* But it also needs couples with a bohemian flair who gather in the illusion of the Parisian café, assuring us that imagination is better when shared. And, finally, it needs Argentinean booksellers.

During the sixties and seventies, La Torre Restaurant and Bar was on the corner of Avenida Ponce de Léon and Avenida Gándara, almost touching the southern border of the university campus. Today there is a Kentucky Fried Chicken, multi-national and impertinent. In the sixties and the beginning of the seventies, it became the confluence for fights and street battles protesting Yankee imperialism and the Vietnam War.

Roberto "El Boquio" Alberty describes those corner confrontations as follows:

> "TEAR GAS"
> Today, I have seen people, so many people
> crying without grief, like in a poetic ode
> as if, on the corner of the University,
> someone had exploded a giant onion
> of hate and thorns.

Coming from Avenida 65 de Infantería, La Torre seemed like an imitation of a Pastrana-style cafeteria, with its modern flair and inedible "self-service" food. The personality of the place was conflicted, fighting to preserve itself as, simultaneously, a Parisian café, a restaurant for the poor, and a bar for alcoholics. The place had a little of everything, as it took in people from every walk of life, like El Boquio and his friend Bonilla, who found their place of power, their place to dream. From the corner of that Río Piedras café, they discussed Breton and Duchamp and dreamed with a European imagination. Bonilla's blackness yearned for the blackness of Frantz Fanon, the little man with the round face, sad look, and glassy eyes, with the paunch of the cirrhotic, who was always a step away from complete self-absorption. He was a tragic clown, but not because of his skin color. The red clown was El Boquio because his imagination always got fired up when mixed with his humor.

Dreaming up her *Animal fiero y tierno* in the poetic landscape of Julia de Burgos, the poet Ángela María Dávila would enter alongside José María Lima, his sandals clacking, his gaze lowered. We couldn't tell if José was considering a mathematical equation for his job or pondering poetic verse for his calling. Like a tropical Alexandrine, or, in other words, in an angle oblique to the rest of the universe, my friend Ché Meléndez would solve some riddle of Borges. As Lezama Lima said, someone flips the switch and out flows Niagara Falls. In Singapore, someone dreams of surrealism and, as a result, you get El Boquio's collages or Bonilla's earnest conversation about how the Marxist philosopher, Althusser, would strangle his wife while giving her a neck massage. Ángela María Dávila accented her blackness with her wild and curly hair, once again resembling Julia. Lima was a mulatto with thick hair, a workingman's mustache, and wearing those African dashikis that would later embarrass us. El Ché also wore sandals and was more of the authentic romantic poet than José María Lima.

Around the early seventies, El Boquio opened his own open-air café. The dream of a Parisian café in the sad and passionate tropics was realized in this café inconveniently located in the alleyway that ran alongside the Paradise Theater. El Boquio's bohemian café was converted from a warehouse reminiscent of the almost attached garage of a Río Piedras Spanish Revival–style home. His gallery served as a place to unleash his imagination while simultaneously making comments from his folding chair. Ruminating over some disappointment, he would emit a terrifying scream, one that sounded like something between the cosmic and the neurotic, while simultaneously lamenting long and hard from his hoped-for "left bank of the Seine"—something he never quite achieved, as his customers would not sit at the open-air tables. El Boquio bewailed the fact that the Puerto Ricans always preferred to be indoors; to eat outside the dining room was unthinkable. I told him it was because of the sun and the harassment from drug addicts. He calmed down when I said the same thing happened under the flowering, yellow oak of El Jibarito Bar and Grill on Calle de Diego. He looked at me with something like neurasthenic incredulity when I told him that the people preferred to sit inside the bar and watch the passersby. The truly Puerto Rican *flâneur* does not fix his gaze on the urban landscape; he is more interested in standing with the other men, sizing them up, his voice rising with every two beers.

Gallagher was the Argentinean bookseller. If in the intellectual formation of García Márquez there had been a magical bookseller in Barranquilla, the bookseller for the literary generation of the seventies was Gallagher. He was our guide along the paths of Hispanic American literature. His bookstore was on Calle González, where today Editiones Huracán publishes books. In the seventies he moved to Avenida Ponce de León, about two or three doors down from La Torre. I still have the collection of Vallejo's poetry he bound for me. Among the books recommended to me was Ernesto Sábato's short masterwork *Tango,* and di Benedetto's novel *Zama,* a mysterious book someone referred me to because of its similarities with *La noche oscura del Niño Avilés.* I remember the day I went to get it. Gallagher was surprised I requested that odd novel. He had recently seen a copy back on the shelves in the depths of the store where the forgotten books reside. Back there the books were in complete disarray. I thought that he would never find *Zama.* However, he returned triumphant. It was the last copy, he would say—he always said the same thing—and, by the worn spine and yellowed pages, I supposed that it was a first edition. It was not a first, though it was an old edition. I told myself that a good bookseller is someone who cares for forgotten books. Gallagher knew where they were because he had handled all of them and read many. He was a short man with the sly look of one from Buenos Aires, and his thick glasses accentuated a lazy eye that only found solace in reading. He came to work in a short sleeve shirt and tie. A kind man, he had a hint of irony toward all that was Puerto Rican, a trait that would have been less easy to take if he had not been married to a happy but ugly Puerto Rican woman. Gallagher was half Irish, and he had a great fondness for Río Piedras. A legendary figure in the formation of a generation of writers and Hispanists, Gallagher cultivated in all of us the desire to become Latin American writers. My passion for the poetry of Vallejo began with him, along with a certain predilection for turning any library into a metaphor for chaos.

I began to appreciate the urban landscape I had known in my adolescence. One of the university *petit maîtres,* who later became a professor and yet another example of the blue culture, in a class one day referred to Emilio Díaz Valcárcel's story "El Sapo en el espejo" with disdain. With a petulant tone and effeminate gestures, he insisted that the story reminded him of the sordid atmosphere of a place like Lugo's on 65 de Infantería. I pointed out that that atmosphere was precisely what posed the biggest challenge for a writer because it had never been dealt with before. To begin to describe a reality is to invent it. Los Angeles, then, would be an invention of Raymond Chandler. At first, the city of letters was indescribable.

From the upper level of the curiously named Pintadera Art Shop, in Eugenio Fernández Granell's "Blue Tower," El Boquio, with long, curly hair like Rafael Alberti and a profile somewhere between that of Breton and Bobby Capó, screamed to the heavens that the Auxilio Mutuo Hospital was more than a borderland between life and death, a no man's land between the street life of Río Piedras, and a Hato Rey in search of its identity. With its "chalet" architecture evoking the Second Empire, the Spanish Society of Auxilio Mutuo was located at the end of the wide, tree-lined avenue. There was something false about the majestic antiquity of its hallways and galleries. But that's not important if we consider the manner in which it made use of the tropical light. The hallways radiated the same creamy, lyrical light with which Van Gogh painted the insane asylum at Arles. I tried to describe that light in *Mujer con sombrero Panamá* before El Boquio foretold from his perch on the "Blue Tower" that the building was like a machine for fabricating shadows, fleeting yet distinct.

The residential complex of El Monte on Avenida Muñoz Rivera, paralleling Ponce de León, expressed the opposite aesthetic or antithesis of that artificial nineteenth-century European style. Flagrantly modernist and inspired by Le Corbusier's concept of the building as a "machine for living," these monstrous buildings, with three hundred apartments each, defined the urban landscape of Hato Rey in 1961. Shaped like an "S" but much more open, their semi-circular architecture lent grace to the first of our bizarre developments.

Through the use of cross ventilation, the colossal two-story buildings achieved an unusual lightness, taking advantage of the afternoon breeze and converting the hallways into exterior galleries with panoramic views of the city in all its narcissistic development. The ample use of the *brise soleil* turned El Monte into a symbol of exceptional economic strength and generous visual appeal with its lush tropical vegetation, its Olympic-size pool, and the white color that would give the new building the elegance of a monument to our modern age.

For my generation born in the late forties, El Monte symbolized a sort of temporary residence where couples who had passed through the first seven years of married bliss would experiment with new modes of matrimony. In furnitureless living rooms with pillows strewn about and under the watchful gaze of a Ché Guevara poster, they had "*craneo* heavy" conversations about open marriages and group sex. El Monte was our very first Villa Pugilato, a place where young professional couples, now part of the corporate grinder, put in their time before heading to the psychiatrist's office or to divorce court. They were all one step away from the chemical dysfunction of the eighties and nineties.

While there, in 1976, I finished *La noche oscura del Niño Avilés*. I wrote the parts about the fugitive city among piles of scattered books, teak drawers, and disassembled bookcases. My only consolation was the three o'clock breeze and the red Fernando de Szyszlo hanging on my white wall. While living in that condo, I attempted my first divorce.

5

Toward the Martín Peña Canal

Hato Rey has always been a drive-through town. There, one finds little of the city's communal memory so often present in its plazas. Perhaps it is for that reason that our minds shift toward the personal, the anecdotal, the tics and irreducible memories whose persistence leaves us perplexed. I remember the Quintana Racetrack with its blue-flowered hedge surrounding the track and stands. There I saw Camarero ridden by Mateo Matos. That memory is juxtaposed with a prior one of how when we used to visit the racetrack my father would tell the story of the horse who, leaving the stables and crossing what is now Calle Mayagüez on his way to the track, stopped and insisted on kicking my father's Dodge with its new whitewall tires.

Later, in the "good ol' days," we would go to the Chicken Inn Restaurant, famed, like El Esquife, for its fried chicken. The famous "Vieja Juliá," the father of Raúl Juliá, hung out in that restaurant. It was there I discovered my first *blanquito perla,* or what my grandmother, Ruperta, called an "old bachelor." Both father and son were theatrical men. The son did well to leave Puerto Rico and not succumb to the adulation of excessively nice, gregarious masculinity.

In the following years the Chicken Inn was converted to a pizzeria, slipping into its own drunken obscurity. That is to say, like the alcoholics who frequented it, the restaurant took the road to despair, eventually collapsing in upon itself. Later it was converted into The Cave of the Chicken Inn, which became a hangout for alcoholics searching for the comforting refuge of its dark interior. Time passes, but, for the patrons inside, it is always night. With its fake Spanish Renaissance décor, The Cave of the Chicken Inn is similar to The Chavales on Roosevelt Avenue. Only glassy and burning eyes are capable of illuminating the depths of a euphoria that always anticipates its own misery. Like fish in the bottom of an aquarium, the men await the time they must return to their wives.

In the same area, running north along Avenida Ponce de León, they built the Banco Popular in 1964. A massive temple, the gray temperance and forceful lines of the bank accentuated its vertical aspirations—like a pin-striped suit. The presence of that enormous vault in Hato Rey would exhaust our sense of awe in the face of a Future guaranteed by Progress. Today our consumerism is greater and our naiveté not quite so manifest. To the south along Ponce de León, the notorious Juliá Clinic, an asylum for the well to do, remains forgotten, lost in the past. In less than a mile, they equated the optimism of bourgeois rationality with the healing of their mental misery. The Banco Popular building would be dedicated to the uncomfortable spirit of a financial and architectural modernity that had not yet found its identity. It did not have the grace of the Caribe Hilton Hotel—constructed thirteen years earlier—nor the international style of Art Deco, popular in the thirties and seen in the Banco Popular in Old San Juan. The building in Hato Rey is like an homage without recognizable architectural signs. At times it seems an exercise in the vanity of the engineers and master architects who proclaim the building's function to the point of boredom. The building has the solemnity of a temple. If the Spanish Renaissance style of the Juliá Clinic disguised the electro-shock therapy within, then here in the new Banco Popular building was outlined a triumphant project, full of itself, without need for apology.

The combination of that building in that precise place where the old Hato Rey train station stood also formed a symbolic crossroad. The construction of a modern, financial San Juan, on top of the former final destination for that remembered train whose windows opened to the landscape of sugarcane plantations as it traveled along our coasts, was seen as a symbolic exchange of old Puerto Rico for the new or of the sugarcane plantation for the single financial "crop" of the famed "936" corporations. Already in the seventies, the establishment of all the banks and financial institutions within the confines of the Monjas slum in Hato Rey and around the central branch of the Banco Popular culminated in the so-called Golden Mile, an ostentatious proclamation that asserted the financial prowess of the new Puerto Rico. It was there that the "high-tech" pharmaceuticals of the "936" would bankroll the fever of a society of consumption, whose values were shifting from the spiritual to the financial and whose new cathedral would be the Plaza of the Americas "Super Mall" located at the western axis of the most powerful bank in Puerto Rico.

As a reminder of a more humble past, the canal remained beneath the Martín Peña Bridge, flowing from El Fanguito, the largest and most miserable slum in Puerto Rico. It was also the canal where Pepe Díaz, "the King of Spain's most valiant man," fought the English in 1797. There, on that bridge, is where Hato Rey ends and Santurce begins. I always thought that the protagonist from José Luis González's short story "En el fondo del caño hay un negrito" lived in one of the shacks that sit almost beneath that bridge.

In one of Jack Delano's photographic expositions where he contrasted the Puerto Rico of the 1940s with modern Puerto Rico, Roberto Sánchez Vilella, then the ex-governor, could not believe that I didn't remember the train that traveled around the island's coasts. I pointed out to him that I was born in 1946, when the train was already on its way out. I also told him that I had a vivid memory of the enormous slum that bordered the canal and of the pestilence that emanated from the notorious El Fanguito.

When José Luis González returned to Puerto Rico in 1973, Nicolás Andreu, the son of César Andreu Iglesias, decided to take a picture of him on one of the two bridges over the canal. As a communist gesture, he wanted the picture to be a sign of his return to Puerto Rico's early realities: the canal, the misery, the immigration from the rural areas to the city, and the capitalist exploitation. José Luis was forty-six and about to be photographed on the Cantera bridge backed by the same dismal background of hovels and stagnant water dotted here and there with palms or almond trees. I don't remember now if it was Nico or José Luis who conceived of that photo as an homage to "En el fondo del caño hay un negrito." José Luis appeared serious, almost grave, surrounded by so much poverty. His face was tilted in its usual manner and that, combined with the beginnings of a double chin, accentuated his gray hair and the sneer that held something of the insolence at the heart of his literary fame. In 1973 I was twenty-six years old, one year short of publishing my first novel. Dressed in a distinguished, long-sleeve *guayabera,* José Luis seemed to me already an old man. As I write this I am fifty-six— ten years older than he was at that time—and I ask myself if my work has a central metaphor as José Luis's work already did back then. And I continue to ask myself why the picture was not taken of José Luis on the Martín Peña Bridge, instead of us having to go to Cantera.

The city also searches for its own metaphors in the canal beneath Martín Peña, dreaming that it stood beside a lagoon, but instead it became a slum that looked out over the bay and northwest to the sea beyond. To the east, moving past the bridge where we photographed José Luis, the city enters the darkness of the mangrove, denouncing its trip to the lagoons of San José and Torrecillas. In *La noche oscura del Niño Aviles* and in *El camino de Yyaloide,* the journey begins toward this lacustrine city that sees itself reflected in the bottom of the canal. My first novel, *La renuncia del héroe Baltasar,* was a story set in the lower promontory of San Juan with a view of the bay. It was a novel about El Morro. Then, I arrived at the idea of diving deeper into that chimerical canal already explored by José Luis. My canal was mythic, going back to the eighteenth century when long boats traveled upon it. The black, Melodía, in *El camino de Yyaloide* was my homage to the child character José Luis drowned in those turbid waters.

6

Santurce, Our Simulacrum of the Big City

The Ubarri train was designed to go over the Cangrejos ridge. You have to close your eyes and visualize the sand pit on the old route between San Juan and Río Piedras. A mythic train, it was built and managed by Count Ubarri of Santurce. Three hills on its promontory gave it a privileged topography overlooking the canals to the south, the bay to the northwest, and the Atlantic to the north. With views to the sea, the bay, and the mangroves, Santurce-Cangrejos was a golden opportunity for a true Puerto Rican city, the panoramic view providing another possible metaphor. If San Juan was the Spanish city high above the Atlantic, sloping gently to the bay, Santurce promised a still greater vista. There, in that place of passage, was hidden the promise of a unique urban landscape.

Every city needs its hills, the watchtowers from which we note its temperament. Navigating the old Ubarri train route beyond the Martín Peña Bridge and through a coconut grove, we discover an essential vision of the past at the crossroad. It's as if there were no other option because the axis of Santurce runs east to west, and we cannot help but climb the first of those hills overlooking the Atlantic.

In Scharneco the street corner disappeared and the confluences were always many as the route from Borinquen Avenue led to the old Barrio Obrero, a working-class neighborhood, which was Puerto

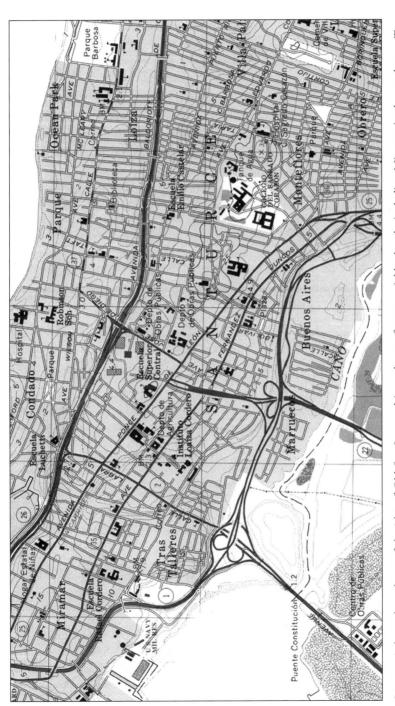

Santurce is located southeast of the islet of Old San Juan and is made up of many neighborhoods, including Miramar in the northwest, Tras Talleres in the center, and Monteflores in the southeast. The working-class neighborhood of Barrio Obrero lies just below Monteflores.

Rican at the beginning of the last century but is now mostly Dominican. It seems in every emigration the poor feel a preference for the old neighborhoods, the ones the city leaves behind. Just at the traffic light where Toño Machuca, the man who laughed like a goat in my novel *Mujer con sombrero Panamá,* was kidnapped, we take a right toward Calle Sagrado Corazón and the Monteflores sector, the first hill of Santurce.

They attacked him there because his secret life was a contradiction between perverse appetites and bourgeois respectability. The man who never drank more than three martinis and who fixed his bow tie every morning felt the desolation of one whose style was in conflict with the Dominican immigration that overwhelmed those streets. Scharneco would reveal that conflict in him, the one that always existed in Santurce: the conflict between the aristocratic and the working class; between the mansions and the projects; between Ubarri, the Count of Santurce, and the black proletariat.

In the fifties, when I really began to understand the neighborhoods of San Juan and the names associated with them, Scharneco held the same contradictions. The place harbored an urban purpose, an unusual thing in the capital because that *chaflán* had a gas station with a cafeteria attached where one could buy excellent *checos,* meat-filled fritters, from Villa Palmeras. *Chaflán* comes from the French *chanfrein* (chamfer). It is a long and narrow surface where, instead of a corner, two faces or flat surfaces join to form an angle. The *checos* were "blind": little meat and mostly air. They are still sold on Avenida Eduardo Conde in Villa Palmeras. Even though the most elegant *chafláns* are in Paris, Times Square is the most famous *chaflán* in the world.

Continuing on the Ubarri train route, we avoid both the working-class and privileged areas of Santurce. Instead, we observe that in this sector of Monteflores the Puerto Rican middle class has achieved some notable architecture. The Las Madres School was built on the western slope, removed from Avenida Ponce de León, as was fitting for an exclusive, Hispanophile school for girls. The main building exhibits architecture of tropical eclecticism from the Belle Epoque where the roofs evoke French culture and the ornate façade native pretension. Traveling to the top of the second hill, the one known as San Mateo, we see mansions that had already lost their appeal by the fifties and sixties sitting one after another. On the corner adjacent to the Las Madres entrance, a furniture store called the Patio Shop was built in the fifties; its ample showcases displayed the furnishings for a new age. We pass some distinguished buildings, such as the School of the Immaculate Conception and the Freemason Grand Lodge, examples of the ambitious architecture with which San Juan occasionally surprises us. And now we arrive at the scenic overlook, the privileged vista. The extraordinary view from atop San Mateo hill signals our euphoria, stealing our breath away as we look over the panorama of Santurce.

The San Mateo Church, located on the hill of the same name, evokes with its sober architecture, simple façade, and two bell towers its ancient dignity as an hermitage. When the English invaded in 1797 it was easy to see, from the heights of San Mateo, the enemy armada extending along the coast. One could also note the need to protect the tranquil waters of the bay on the south side of Cangrejos. It was a vulnerable place we nearly called the *patria* because in 1797 the Puerto Ricans were still Creoles, mainly of Spanish descent. The San Mateo hermitage, located in a solitary, deserted area, had been used as a chapel by travelers. It was later converted into a lookout post, a place to spy the Atlantic threat, the alien empire positioning itself in the Caribbean to lay siege to the rumored secrets of the mangroves, canals, and mountains and hills beyond the bay. It is important to understand the particular emotion one feels when confronting the sea and its inner searchings, to have the certainty of a prayer atop a wasteland with a view of the coconut forest below.

In the city, time is not simply historical; it is scarcely linear. Memory coincides in the space of different epochs. Below, halfway down the slope of San Mateo, at stop 24 on Avenida Ponce de León, around the year 1957, stood the Metropolitan Theater. That corner exemplified modernity, specifically, the modernity of the nocturnal city. While on clear afternoons the façade of San Mateo kept vigil, awaking in us a better appreciation for the light of the city, that corner, illuminated by the glowing neon lights of the Metropolitan Theater, provided evidence of the excitement and seduction of the present moment. To arrive in the evening with the expectation of seeing *The Ten Commandments* or *Ben-Hur* and to anticipate afterwards the certainty of the city at night, the obligatory walk past the window displays, and the proximity of El Nilo Diner at stop 22 was to feel genuinely fortunate.

I always imagined Santurce at night. To enter El Nilo and climb to the mezzanine was to pass through a glowing, yellow light that illuminated the clamor in the place. What impressed me were the neat hats worn by the waiters behind the bar and the starched waistcoats of the servers. Far from an Aguas Buenas cafeteria or the Pastrana family's Don's on the 65 de Infantería, I felt the euphoria of the city. Santurce exuded something of the foreign. I had to travel to Europe in order to find a similar sensation, the feeling of entering a place overflowing with city life, without a trace of the desolation that goes along with the small-town cafeteria or the roadside bar.

Looking toward Avenida de Diego from stop 22, the sidewalks became Parisian boulevards, with trees blowing in the breeze from the nearby sea. There, we would feel ourselves in the true heart of modern San Juan. Facing El Nilo, the Art Deco of the Banco Popular provided visible evidence of the "Metropolis" whose Professional Building, constructed on de Diego, used to be the tallest in Puerto Rico, a sort of provincial skyscraper. Santurce was pedestrian, noisy, and nocturnal. I recall that as we entered El Nilo my father pointed to El Chévere across the street, telling us emphatically that back in the forties, when he arrived looking for work in Santurce, he remembered having seen the poet Lloréns Torres at a literary gathering in that very restaurant. He had to explain to me that Lloréns Torres was someone honored by the housing project. In Santurce, my father tracked famous people, those with names that resonated. In El

Nilo, I asked for a "banana split." For a boy raised in a town with three streets, the name had an exotic enchantment.

Santurce was the simulacrum of our Caribbean city, its pedestrian traffic hustling both day and night, and always there was the proximity of the street, the neighborhood, and the Avenue. But there was also the corner under the flickering light, a magnet for the restless. Further down, near the notorious Club 22, on the corner of the old Puerto Rico Theater where the Bellas Artes Center sits today, mythic encounters took place between the young Rafael Cortijo and the famous whore chaser, Benny Moré. It was said that when they visited San Juan they followed the Antillean music all the way to the neighborhoods where the music sounded. Back then the ties between Cuba and Puerto Rico had not yet been cut by the Cuban Revolution. We can imagine a corner jam session in the Minillas neighborhood with a character dressed in a long-sleeve *guayabera,* flamboyantly smoking his cigar, his romantic song invigorated by the rhythm of the bongos and the *marímbola,* that crate bass tuned with metal hoops and invented in working-class streets.

And an Avenida Ponce de León lit up by the city is best shot on nights when it drizzles incessantly because then the neon lights and the headlights of the slowly moving cars reflect simultaneously off the pavement, the windows, and the chrome. Close your eyes and the boy sees that black Dodge with the whitewalls; the city is inhabited by ghost cars, a 1950 chromium-plated Ford à la Boston Blackie.

We continue our route to San Juan and further down, at stop 20, is Central High, also designed by Rafael Carmoega. And in front, in that same corner, the Georgetti mansion was erected. The González Padín department store, across from Central High, in the late fifties boasted the first escalator in Puerto Rico. There were up to four recognizable historic styles in such a small urban space and that's if we count the timid Art Deco style of the old telegraph building. Each style represented a particular decade of the last century through the fifties: Frank Lloyd Wright's prairie house style, as envisioned by Antonin Nechodoma (seen in the Georgetti mansion); the Spanish

Renaissance style, with its dignified neo-classical columns that Carmoega wanted for Central High; the tropical Art Deco style of the thirties; and that somewhat anonymous architecture brought in with the fifties that flaunted a generic modernity.

There, at bus stop 20, but on the side of Fernández Juncos, my father used to take his Pontiac with its leather interior every Saturday to the Shell station in front of La Borincana. For me, La Borincana was the Saturday restaurant par excellence. Even at eleven years old, I understood that restaurants had uniformed waiters and eateries had locals with rolled-up sleeves recruited to shout the menu of the day over grim faces and the stink of sweat.

Stop 20 also accessed the Plaza del Mercado in Santurce. Since my father worked in the federal building on Calle Canals, he knew when and where the famous people gathered. He knew all the eateries and told me where he used to see the poet Luis Palés Matos talk and drink. If memory serves me, it was some place near the Plaza de Mercado, on the street with the French name, Duffaut, which runs into Ponce de León at the old health department building. That was Palés Matos's territory because he would also go near the Paramount Theater to the Palace Diner where you sat surrounded by the caricatures of star actors and musicians like Diplo, Myrta Silva, Sylvia Rexach, and José Luis Torregrosa. Santurce had the vanity of a big city. Some of the people who passed through were notorious, many of its buildings noteworthy.

In his book *Techo a dos aguas,* the poet José Luis Vega describes Santurce's Plaza de Mercado as a place that contains the surprise of a literary history: "The Santurce Plaza, on the other hand, surrounded by an urban environment, had a more public spirit, a spirit more authentically Puerto Rican in the manner of Tomás Blanco, a spirit that was more literary. In those surroundings, José I. de Diego Padró and Luis Palés Matos exercised their talent as Antillean *flâneurs* as well as the bohemian myth of their alcoholism." The fame of a city also rests in its literary avenues. In this sense, San Juan is not, as some have said, a city without merit.

We arrive at stop 18 on the Condado side, searching for the Luchetti School, the poor, native version of the Labra School, which boasts strong bricks, Yankee Puritanism, and a neo-classical style halfway between a church and a penitentiary. We arrive in the land dreamed up by Magali García Ramis in *Felices Días, Tío Sergio* and by José Luis González in *La luna no era de queso.* Both are autobiographical books. The first is a novel that nourishes memory and the second is composed of memories made into a novel. Both deal with a Santurce somewhere between the city neighborhoods and the suburbs, the simulacrum of a city threatened by dispersion. It is a rumor close to truth. In the case of *Felices Días, Tío Sergio,* the suburban developments have not yet arrived, though they are approaching. The city neighborhoods are also threatened in the memoirs of José Luis González, and though he didn't foresee the developments, he did describe a Guaynabo that was both rural and upper class. In both books the city neighborhoods of Santurce are presented as superior modes of living, though they are besieged by rumors of the suburban developments that would diminish their enchantment. Near stop 18, where the fast-food restaurant China Sun sits today with its twenties style Shanghai architecture, stood Matías Photo Shop in 1957, where on our Saturday excursions we bought baseball magazines and *Classics Illustrated,* those comic books that depicted great literary works.

Don Juan Antonio Corretjer's Socialist League was located right off stop 15. It was an organization feared by the police and destroyed by amatory gossip. One Thursday night I went to visit them. I was about to graduate from the university and was able to understand something of why the Socialist League had to be located in that working-class neighborhood frequented by prostitutes where Avenida Fernández Juncos ran into Tras Talleres and what was called Corona then climbed toward Avenida Ponce de León, where record distributors and recording studios were located. It was not easy to find the Socialist League. I got lost in that sordid building. I climbed to the terrace only to find a scene that I have understood ever since to be a noble representation of my profession. A man I assumed was a writer sat typing, gazing out the terrace window. I imagined he was César Andréus Iglesias with whom I always identified. He might have been an accountant, but I wanted him to be a writer. He had long hair, which alone seemed to indicate he was no accountant. On the terrace, everything was dark except for the yellow light shining from the desk lamp. I wanted to have the same ability to concentrate that this man had as he sat absorbed in intellectual thought. If I wrote at night, I would aspire to that quiet meditation. At any rate, that night, while leaving the Socialist League with Juan Antonio Corretjer and Carmín Pérez, I witnessed one of those displacements of the poet toward the pretentious sweetness of social realism. In the cafeteria and confectionary on the corner, Corretjer, whose expressions were always difficult to decipher, pointed out to Pérez the sumptuous sale of sweets and cakes. He assured her that under socialism, nobody, least of all the poor children, would have to look with their noses stuck on the display case at such abundance.

The third hill in old Santurce used to be called Olimpo; it is known today as Miramar. A neighborhood of architectural distinction in an authentically Puerto Rican style with a hint of the uppity Vedado neighborhood in Havana, Miramar is a city neighborhood closed to outsiders, discreet in the silence of its sidewalks and streets. It is a place without high walls, even though it is inclined toward the exclusivity of the bourgeoisie. Inhabited since the early twentieth century, privileged in some areas with views of the Condado Lagoon or the Atlantic and in other areas with a view of the bay, Miramar is a high-class neighborhood—what Monteflores used to be. The architecture is in the style of Ponce, more island-like than peninsular, but without that rhetorical, new bourgeois touch of the "regal" Ponce of the nineteenth century. The money flaunted here does not seem to be the result of commercial agricultural exportation, but rather the fruits of a prosperous, professional bourgeoisie in search of and in possession of a territory recently discovered and endowed with the gift of various vistas of the coastal landscape.

Miramar also exhibits a literary imagination. In *El manuscrito de Miramar,* the writer Olga Nolla places us in spaces of amorous secrets and clandestine correspondences, where, like the streets of Miramar, the lives of high-class women are necessarily hidden in existential discretion. That novel has as its focus the two sides of the city: the big house in Miramar that hears the rumor of its approaching destruction and the memory that recalls a city university of *petit maîtres* and libidinous professors whose biographies are suggested in code. Its unmistakable mark is that of the bourgeois neighborhood, of life lived behind closed doors, discretely, in the long silence that is memory.

If Olga Nolla achieved a landscape of interior streets in *El manuscrito de Miramar,* the Miramar of the poet Hjalmar Flax contains definitive signs of the place, signs only a poet can offer. It is easy to recognize Flax walking the streets of Miramar with the territorial stateliness of a dandy. His somewhat baroque attire begins with a jacket that he always wears, even under the red-hot sun. His hat and white beard complete his persona, without forgetting, of course, the Ray-Ban sunglasses and the thermos of distilled water that he puts on the table in the Arcos restaurant—in the lower level of the Hotel Toro—where he always gets the bargain plate of chicken with rice. To the perplexity of the Dominican waitress, Flax always asks for a glass without ice—it would ruin his distilled water. Hjalmar Flax would seem to be a *flâneur,* one who does not take pleasure in brandy yet obsesses over bottled water.

In his poem "Cerebración del vicionario," he celebrates the close proximity of the condos and buildings in Miramar, which turns the city neighborhood into a somewhat indiscriminate accomplice in the assault of one's privacy. The unusual burlesque of the poem reminds us of that urban painting by Edward Hopper that shows the possibility of the voyeur who, lonely and introspective, examines the solitary look that finds intimacy without revealing vulnerability:

> Beyond your morality and your myopia
> Venus and poetry are born in Santurce,
> At times, from the most banal vices.

61

Occasionally the dandy enters into the frustrations of a gentle-
man who lived in Miramar in an apartment—designed by Henry
Klumb, with a view of the bay, the Abarca Foundry, and the dikes—
that had seen better times.

> He left a note in the mailbox
> The man who knows how to fix
> The intercom.
> He says, in few words, that
> The contacts have been eaten
> By the humidity, by the salt,
> That the apparatus is obsolete

In other moments Miramar and its bay unfolds before us in the
verses of this extraordinary poet, in the promise of a panorama that
disappears as soon as it is seen, like the most lyric of poetry:

> At this instant, the morbid bay
> coagulates in metal where two boats
> cross, magnetic and silent,
> great tapestries of sun like crystals
> fall, are smashed to bits, splinters ricochet,
> passing through pupils at the same
> speed as light. When the hand
> tries to raise itself, you are already blind.

7

Road to the Bohemian Lights

Without delay, I embarked on another San Juan experience, taking in its urban landscape from a *guagua* (bus); for the moment, my destination was Santurce. I avoided sitting in "the kitchen," those seats over the rear motor, because that is where the dispossessed sat staring at the vomit of heroin addicts and drunks. I took a seat in the middle, preferring isolation and the company of the solitary and vice ridden, the people who keep no schedule, as opposed to the workers at rush hour. From the bus, the city was a faithful companion. I rarely spoke to those sitting next to me. My interest turned toward the sidewalk, guessing at the life stories of each of the passersby. The *flâneur* is also a prophet of perfect stories.

The first time I took the bus through Santurce I was going to the Paramount Theater. They were showing *Five Pennies,* the biography of Red Nichols, starring Danny Kaye. Once I was initiated into the curiosities of adolescence, I adventured more toward San Juan. At the Lorraine, before it became just another porn theater where men went to beat off, I saw the biography of Gene Krupa, starring Sal Mineo. By then I was into playing the drums and contemplating the mysteries of tobacco.

When my father and I arrived at the nearly deserted Escambrón Beach Club, where the San Juan Jazz Workshop played its Sunday

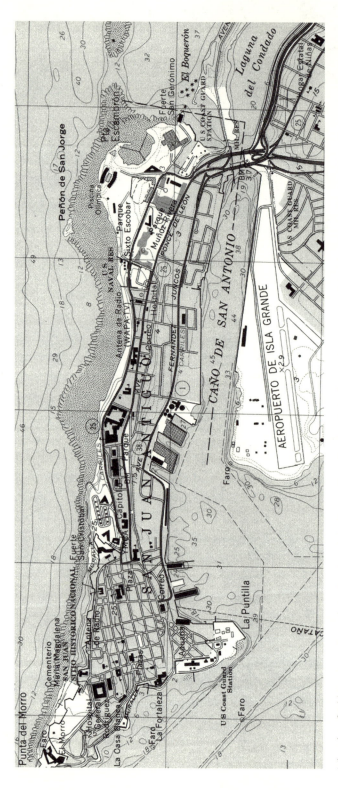

The islet of Old San Juan. Escambrón Beach and the Parque Sixto Escobar lie in the northeast corner of the islet. Parque Muñoz Rivera lies just below the Parque Escobar. The Normandie Hotel and the Caribe Hilton Hotel cannot be seen on the map but lie on the eastern shore of the islet next to San Gerónimo Fort. San Cristóbal Fort lies on the north shore just east of the old town—note that the capitol lies just below it. Also note the location of El Morro (referred to by Rodríguez Juliá as the "Campo del Morro") on the northwest tip of the islet.

concerts—according to my father, I was too young to be going to smoky nightclubs—I remembered Bob "El Múcaro" Thurman's foul balls in Sixto Escobar Park. In the forties and fifties, the Escambrón Beach Club, the Sixto Escobar Park, and the Muñoz Rivera Park had a promiscuous relationship where legends hung out together and myths were shared. I remember holding my father's hand, going to the Caribbean Series of 1958, and the fact that we had to sit in general admission because there were no reserved seats. I felt the passage of time like a sudden blow, like the solitary crocodile under the pines in Muñoz Rivera Park that was hit by one of Thurman's baseballs. Of all the legends of Sixto Escobar Park, with its view of the pines and the Atlantic Ocean, the most treasured was that of a certain member of the "Panic Squad of 1954"—Willie Mays, Bob Thurman, George Crowe, Willard Brown, and the rookie Roberto Clemente— who hit his homeruns only at night. When one speaks of Joshua Gibson and Frank "Condominium" Howard and how they knocked balls all the way from stop 8 over the pines, past the scoreboard with the Don Q emblem, and out to sea, Thurman's feat—waking up the inhabitants of the zoo that was never completed in Muñoz Rivera Park—becomes a most oneiric or fantastic act, something imagined by a Magritte with a tropical bowler hat.

That afternoon, at twilight, I contemplated the Escambrón Beach for the first time. Later we entered a dance hall with a strong, musty smell. As there was hardly anyone around, I screwed up the courage to enter into a discussion with my father that was both pointless and forced. They started playing modern jazz, and I explained to my father that the "rim shot," invented by Jimmy Cobb, was used to accentuate the rhythm by laying the stick across the rim of the drum. He looked at me perplexed, the intelligence of an agronomic engineer with a government post overwhelmed by the obsessive eccentricities of my adolescence.

Later, my bohemian nature led me to go out alone at night to the concerts put on by the San Juan Jazz Workshop in La Botella in front of the San José Plaza. My obsession was modern jazz, and my ambition was to chart the bohemian nightlife throughout the city. But first I had to pass by the Sixto Escobar, recalling my infancy, reliving my childhood, seeing once again that creamy light beyond the pines—that three-in-the-afternoon light in the mountains of Aguas Buenas with their clean profile seen from the seats at Solá Morales ballpark—that light of "Three Kings' Day" that clears the winter air, allowing me to see all the greens of the mountains both far and near.

I would pass by the beach near stop 8 and ask myself if it were possible that a baseball hit by Josh Gibson or Frank Howard could bounce off that sea-swept reef in the same way Thurman's balls bounced off the crocodile's skin. Later we would pass by Puerta de Tierra, where the old colonial buildings, like the officer's club, gave the neighborhood an aura of secrecy. Those federal buildings seemed like remnants from World War II, having survived their purpose of vigilance. Near San Juan and past the National Guard building there begins a succession of institutional buildings that make no secret of their purpose, placed so as to take in the entire panorama from the breakwater all the way to the promontory of Bajamar.

Bajamar has a rocky beach and a headland that from above could be mistaken for walls. It is the place where the old city tests the temperament of its light, sometimes clear to the horizon, other times hazy, sedated by the salty air. At times the white foam of the crashing waves, the surges and swells, create a harmony with the light. Other times the stillness extends the view, our hearing absorbed by the gentle rolling of the sea. It was here I saw the sea for the first time, exactly at the promontory facing the capitol. It is also the view that I imagined Luis Palés Matos had when he wrote these lines from the poem "El Llamado":

> Today, I remember, is a fortunate day
> of cloudless skies and pure earth:
> erratic swallows
> dot the blue calm.
> I face the sea and in the distance
> the wing of a sail wanes,

> disappears,
> and I, also, erasing myself in it.
> When in the end I return
> by a slight glimmer of conscience,
> how far I am from myself!
> What a strange world surrounds me!

It is exactly these qualities, the ones seen and the ones dreamed of once we spy the fort of San Cristóbal, which turn the entrance to San Juan into our own intimate experience under its unique light.

The old medical school, with its Moorish, plateresque, Spanish Revival style, was once known as the school of "Medicina Tropical." In addition to the study of *bilharzia* or Schistosomiasis and other diseases characteristic to this latitude, there was the coincidence of the tile roof with the palms, the Ficus, and the almond trees, all of which lent an air of exotic fantasy, as if rethinking the road to the Alhambra from a promontory with a view of the seashore lined with coconut groves. Because all of the buildings, including Carmoega's capitol, which served as the backdrop on my first visit to the sea, have their somewhat generic backs gazing out at the Atlantic, the façades are, with great effort, a succession of distinct historic moods from the colonial city, its historicist synecdoche, our Hall of Lost Steps.

The capitol, surpassed in classical ambition by Washington, its dome not quite so spiked as the dome in Havana, runs into Casa de España, in which the garish Spanish Renaissance becomes a fake, the lion fountain more a gesture to Disneyworld than to the Alhambra. Even so, the building preserves a past, even a recent past, which confers dignity. The Ateneo Puertorriqueño, or Puerto Rican Athenaeum, is scarcely a stone's throw away from here, its sober façade barely visible from the height of the promontory of San Cristóbal.

The other buildings, like the Carnegie Library, the old YMCA, and the Center for Government Receptions, with both Belle Epoque and Porfirista aspects, constitute a collection of our provincial, eclectic architecture. The classical and palatial proportions are better seen in the current Olympic headquarters and the Carnegie Library, perhaps an homage to Jeffersonian, Yankee sobriety. In the middle of such colonial ostentation is the Puerto Rican Athenaeum: its façade, with Moorish arcades and Damascene ornamentation, never reaches the Spanish narcissism of the Casa de España. Its beauty lies in the fact that it makes no announcement of its ancestry, preserving an authentically Puerto Rican discretion. Interestingly, they held receptions in the Casa de España for officials from the German fleet that visited our port back in the second half of the 1930s, a little before the Great War. Many of the *petit maîtres* that raised their arm in the Falangist salute during those receptions would later become the usual suspects in the myth of throwing Judge Enjuto from the university tower.

To enter the old quarter of San Juan is to understand, almost immediately, the promise of the neighborhood, of lives led in proximity, of indiscretions veiled by shutters, of rumors heard through partition walls and in entryways. If this New World city, as much Spanish as Puerto Rican, had one ambition, it would be the stroll. It was always the dream of the old quarter, after existing for centuries as a military bastion. The city often yearned for Europe as its model, particularly in its vision of the Madrid boulevards. In its ambition to become a great city, overcome its neurasthenic provincialism, and cure the sadness and boredom of these latitudes, the walled city endured a sort of Madame Bovary existence.

Santiago Plaza, today called the Plaza Colón, the entrance to the old quarter, would be an obvious manifestation of that unconfessed ambition. When I came to San Juan by bus in the sixties, Plaza Colón was the last stop. I never imagined that the Tapia Theater, on the left, was an homage to a writer who also was a chronicler of the city. In *Mis memorias,* Alejandro Tapia y Rivera tells us:

> Before the new theatre was built, Santiago Plaza was an open space, which the building of the theatre greatly improved. Surrounded with granite benches, covered by beautiful almond trees, its center was paved with concrete. That is how I discovered it, and, still a child, it was there I witnessed the great congregation of masks of

every social class as, every Sunday afternoon from San Juan to Santa Rosa, they went in search of consolation to the beat of the military band playing there in the downtown area. It was then, as a result of this carnival, that the place was named El Prado as a distant reminder of the famous Paseo del Prado in Madrid.

We climb to the right toward Boulevard del Valle, and we note how the city is divided into two parts: the high section with a panoramic view of the Atlantic, and below, the streets near the port, where the spectacular view turns intimate, shadowed by the presence of the mountains that cut through the horizon on the other side of the bay. Climbing, still, toward Boulevard del Valle, our goal is the hill by the sea and the light that blinds and bewilders, light of such strength that we ultimately turn away.

Much later, in my inebriated years, I spent many hours in Amanda's Restaurant, at the intersection of Sol with Boulevard del Valle. Yes, I remained catatonic before that panorama, seated outside, burnt by the island sun until I appeared mulatto. Yes, I appeared almost black in the photo Manolo took of me there at Amanda's with a double margarita sitting on a little cement ledge. Manolo served margaritas to his one-eyed dog and blew beatific smoke in her nostrils only to return to the kitchen to shoot craps with Eggie-Joe, the cook. Without even a cigarette, I would remain catatonic for hours, condemned to a stone-faced sadness. Manolo's one-eyed bitch would get drunk and fall belly-up at my feet. I was scarcely able to smile.

But there was another, earlier time when Old San Juan seemed to push my neurasthenic buttons. In my youth, after reading Pedro Salinas's book of poems entitled *El Contemplado,* the city's light was extinguished for me. It manifested itself as an obsessive caress, the idée fixe of being unable to reach the heights of that light over Boulevard del Valle, incapable of penetrating that blissful and beatific glare. In Manuel Hernández Acevedo's *naif* paintings, I could discern that light in the skies of La Perla, the small kites caught in the crossbeams of the light posts on this side of that blue Fra Angelico, which the Boulevard offers on the glorious days clear of the fickle salty air or the rare sand that has traveled from the distant Sahara. I could only see the San Juan light, that culmination of sea and sky, through the painting or grieve for it in front of the building located opposite La Perla, where decades later there would be tennis shoes and stuffed dolls hanging from the electrical poles.

That post-colonial building—constructed in the thirties and eaten away over time by the salty air until, by the fifties, it was destroyed—would end up as a hostel for single men. It was there I fled from the light. I suppose seeing a picture of Pedro Salinas dressed in white contributed to my obsession. I wrote a prose poem entitled "Cuando los hombres vestían de blanco," returning to that time before my birth, an age when the light over the city was even more evident. A good part of my youth was spent searching for the certainty of that light. During the time I visited Amanda's with Manolo, my attempt to hide from the light yielded to Lady Catatonia.

It was also a search for the marine skyline. The light yearned for that encounter beyond La Perla with all its miseries: the flags of the political parties that changed every four years, the memory of having been a slaughterhouse in the old city buried now under the prosperous slum with its young people high on crack, a melodramatic place of passing in René Marqués's *The Oxcart*. My fixation was altogether different. It has already been mentioned how the peasants yearned to leave the fields for the city neighborhoods only to end up in the slums. My haunts were suspended over the clouds low in the sky, distracting me from the horizon in *Allende de los mares*. This xylography by Rafael Tufiño shows a woman seated on one of the benches on Boulevard del Valle. She has a baby in her arms and is contemplating the horizon; below her is the entrance to La Perla. The woman dreams of some distant city, though her housecoat and bare feet belie the hustle and bustle of the San Juan neighborhood. At any rate, there is something like Madame Bovary in the image, as if by searching so long beyond the sea she would remember the father of the creature in her arms. Suddenly, everything has become domestic and vulgar. But, like Baudelaire in "The Clouds," I continue searching for the inverted cities that hang from the sky, the neurasthenia of light, the certainty of imagination.

The veil obscuring the light and the blindfolds covering my eyes brought me nearer to that dark place of the imagination. Arriving in Ballajá, where before there had been a complete neighborhood contained within the city but later they had built magnificent buildings like the Beneficencia Asylum and the Barracks, we note that Tapia—Puerto Rico's first man of letters—recalled something that went back to the eighteenth century: the search for the dreamed city. It was the San Juan of the painter Campeche, a melancholic man, aficionado of billiards, organist in the Cathedral, creator of our first image. That San Juan was a place imagined by our first man of letters: "Before I was born, or a little after, a wood theater existed along with what is today the Military Hospital in a manor house that was part of the hospital; it was a true 'Comedy Corral,' as they were called in some cities in Spain. I'd heard about it from word of mouth."

He foretold that eighteenth-century San Juan, and I imagined it fettered by the picaresque peninsula. When I wrote *La noche oscura del Niño Avilés,* I pitched the territory of my imagination in the Campo del Morro, in the canals that run from the bay to Vacía Talega, and in the high reaches of Ballajá. They were three invisible cities in search of their own identity, perhaps something in between being an official chronicler of the "Siglo de las Luces," the "Century of Lights," and a rogue in the manner of Quevedo's hero in *El buscón.* That sort of slyness is difficult to recognize through the centuries. Tapia's testimony is a distant echo of our ancient vulgarity: "In as much as the famous satires of Ramón de La Cruz didn't lack in extravagance, they occasionally drew upon the local flavor. According to the title of one such farce, attributed to the pen of Cándamo, one could judge our public aesthetic at that time. He named it literally: 'Wake in Ballajá and turmoil in black ass.'"

And Tapia adds toward the sixth decade of the nineteenth century: "A title that wouldn't dare be displayed on corner posters today."

It was Campeche's prophecy and a certain obscure, Piranesi-style vision. In *La renuncia del héroe Baltasar,* the Campo del Morro had already been the "Garden of the Unfortunate"; now it would be the site of a visionary city, an aerial labyrinth of disproportionate towers, foul-smelling swamps, and rooms with oppressive ceilings, like the attics in old mansions, a mix of Fellini in the *Satyricón,* the engravings of Piranesi, and the cover of Miles Davis's *Bitches Brew.* The Campo del Morro, that promontory that kept vigil over the entrance to the bay, looking like an enormous, seemingly stranded ship, was a blank canvas for twilight visions. If the city denied me its diaphanous light, it was time to return its children to Saturn.

The bistro La Botella remained on the corner, in front of the Rodríguez Military Hospital parking lot, where the now vanished neighborhood of Ballajá stood at the end of the eighteenth century. La Botella was the twin of Sam's Patio; it had a French flair on account of the fact that it was painted in tones of red, green-gray, yellow, and black. Instead of hamburgers like they had at Sam's Patio, La Botella had live jazz. When I was seventeen, to visit old San Juan was to make a pilgrimage to the progressive jazz concerts in that bar filled with smoke and sandal-wearing gringos stranded in the tropics. It was an intoxicated cave where Nancy Johnson played alongside Joe Zambrana and a Monchito Muñoz almost sleeping over his cymbals. I imagined it as a cave of beatniks; I did not know that it was a bohemian place for gringo *pieds noirs* who worked in the editorial office of the *San Juan Star* and who would later become famous writers, such as: William Kennedy, who wrote *Ironweed,* and Hunter S. Thompson, author of *Rum Diary.* Toward the mid-sixties, La Botella was restored, losing part of its old enchantment: the dark bar, the always-open leaf doors, the high ceilings, and an ambience of failure hovering over the tables. Tufiño captured in a xylograph and also in a silk screen the moment when Charlie Rodríguez started playing the sax and Monchito Muñoz woke up, or at least nearly did. A little further down, in El Batey, Hunter S. Thompson probably met Luis Muñoz Lee, the son of Muñoz Marín and the editor of *The Island Times*. Like El Farolito in *Under the Volcano,* the place was a dive where the neurasthenia of the failed did not allow for the consolation of music. There, people drank in the gringo way. The alcoholic fumes could make your nerves explode, like the time in the late seventies when William Storryck, my swimming guru, wanted to fight with me by the eighth drink. As a matter of fact, I am sure that we went to drink, but I don't remember now if it was in El Batey or in the Small World Bar that his complex over his five-foot-eight frame blew out of proportion. Sam's Patio, La Botella, and El Batey were the territories of Mr. Danger.

Calle del Cristo was also the territory of René Marqués. His imagination needed that urban landscape of the past in order to find his tone and vision. In the forties and fifties, Old San Juan was still working class, residential; the restored patios would come later. Like the Havana of today, its secret inclination was toward ruin. The past was suspended in dust. The mix of urine, the grime of a Galician warehouse, and the omnipresent garlic scent defined the aroma of the city. Only ghosts, memories of a bourgeoisie that probably moved to Miramar, inhabited those half-destroyed mansions. Similar works like *Purificación en la Calle del Cristo* and *Los soles truncos* found their atmosphere in that side street that ends at the Santo Cristo de la Salud Chapel, discovering the sadness of a past that can only be recovered in nostalgia and resentment. A nationalist leader, Pedro Albizu Campos, lived at the corner of Sol and Cruz and would find in *Una ciudad llamada San Juan* the unnamable sensation of an oppressive past, one in which the ancient roofs and walls will become a sentence of desperation, defeat, and political pessimism.

When Emilio S. Belaval returns to that ancient territory in *Cuentos de la Plaza Fuerte,* he turns the city into an occasion for baroque prose and mystery. The walled cityscape is a mythic space, an investigation of history through legend: "The narrow side streets along Calle Tetuán were the lair of that tar siren who would thrash her tail demoniacally when she lay in the arms of men, and who was ready to wait for her betrothed until the stars faded from the headlands." The baroque, elliptical style portrays a historic and legendary time. The narration is entitled "Biography" and it is as if we experienced that voice through a science-fiction trip to the past. In 1974, forty years after the publication of *Cuentos de la Plaza Fuerte*, I wanted to publish my novel written two years earlier, which also sought that identity revealed in the antiquity of the city. My novel, *La renuncia del héroe Baltasar*, is also written in the spirit of consolation that the past bestows. At any rate, I had been convinced of the impossibility of describing Avenida 65 de Infantería, better to write only stories and legends from the past, like that of Baltasar Montañez and the horse races held on Calle del Cristo, a past that would be capable of redeeming the Progress to which the Estado Libre Asociado (ELA), or Commonwealth, of Puerto Rico has condemned us.

In 1964 the proletariat of Old San Juan began to move toward a Progress that was within reach, just on the other side of the bay. Pedro Juan Soto spoke to us about that moment when the suburbs and the desire of those who were determined to "progress" would displace the city of René Marqués and Emilio S. Belaval. Though Soto was not from an aristocratic family like Marqués, he still felt nostalgia for a past of ancient and noble mansions. In *Ardiente suelo, fría estación,* Soto satirized that place to which many poor families in Old San Juan aspired:

> Only the façades were distinct. Six or seven styles had been distributed geometrically between both sides . . . In front of one, situated in the middle of the block, they stopped.
> "Levittown," Eduardo said, on the way down.

Ironically, Levittown was also the promised land of the Puerto Ricans returning from New York, the "Nuyoricans." Those with both round-trip and one-way tickets found a common destination in the suburb on the other side of the bay. It was just the opposite of my New Venice.

The old quarter of San Juan slopes down to the bay. The corner of Calle San Justo, situated on the hillside in the old Santa Bárbara neighborhood, has one of the best views of the Atlantic, surprising us with its *trompe l'oeil* perspective because, like a dream, the ships anchored in the wharf seem to continue up onto the street. It is as if the ships had gauged their speed incorrectly and had run aground, stranded in the middle of the city.

The construction of the old quarter at the bottom of the hill presents an intriguing curiosity as the city was always trying to keep the rainwater from running down the hillside and out into the bay, causing sedimentation. The solution was to convert San Juan into a city of flat roofs and cisterns. They would collect the rainwater before it ran down the hill. That is why the aerial view of San Juan is markedly different from that of Havana or Cartagena de Indias. Those cities flaunt tiled, inclined roofs that seem older than ours, reminiscent of the sixteenth century. The location of our city required us to live with the problem of the rains, which we resolved with roofs that give our city a certain veiled symmetry, as if the military engineers had always kept watch over practical necessities.

It's a privileged view we have from atop the city. The panorama, which was celebrated by our first well-known painter, José Campeche, in his portrait of governor Ustáriz, became bound to the symbols, changes, and uncertainties of the old city. In his representation, Campeche showed the paving of the streets. We were on our way to solving the problem of the water and mud running down the hill. Here was where the picturesque landscape of Puerto Rico began. In the background of the painting, following the course of the street, we see the bay, the San Antonio canals, the marshes of Miraflores and beyond, and the hills of the north coast. We feel the intimacy of the bay. It is like the first representation of the island home, of the *patria,* and the sensation that we have is one of boundaries reached by the peacefulness of nature converted into scenery, of vulnerability before history.

The historical city also contains the lettered city of bohemian gatherings and friendships. Its spiritual call includes testimonies to the ability of sharing the intellectual and the artistic life.

On the lower part of the hill, by Calle del Cristo, we turn to the right and pass the shady, solitary corners of Caleta de San Juan, a street that ends in a small pier, thus *caleta,* or "small bay." It is one of the few San Juan streets with tree-lined sidewalks. The nearness to the Puerta de San Juan at one end of the street combined with the ceremonial atrium of the cathedral on the opposite was surely the reason that this old-quarter neighborhood merited a different shade than was granted by the two-story buildings.

Now, as we stand before the Puerta de San Juan, the voices of the bohemian world of the twenties and thirties call to us. We suspend our investigation into the distant past of the city and move forward in time to a recent past made up of voices and ethereal figures, what the poet Hugo Gutiérrez Vega called (I do not remember if he was referring to Salvador Novo) Art Deco people. In *Luis Palés Matos y su trasmundo poético* we have one of the most complete testaments to an age where some of the most illustrious names in politics and literature walked the streets of Old San Juan with a carefree attitude and adolescent gaiety, their childish pranks matching the heights of their talent. In one of the greatest testimonials in our literature, José I. de Diego Padró describes for us that moment made up of unforgettable places and people whose names have been taken by the public housing projects, such as Lloréns Torres. He tells us how he and Palés Matos—the founders of the poetic vanguard movement known as "Diepalismo"—went fishing at night by La Puntilla in the marina or in the Puerta de San Juan: "Once we got the bug to go fishing, we would spend the entire afternoon at La Puntilla in the marina buying *mojarras* or sardines for bait—they usually gave them to us. And as night fell, there we were, Palés and I, never far from

76

the pier or the Puerta de San Juan, with our lines flat over the foamy water."

Later he describes the foolishness that today we associate with another age because, not unlike the young *petit maîtres* of the twenties, these bohemians turned their pranks into a sort of initiation for a literary brotherhood: "One night a shower of rocks came loose near us accompanied by mocking voices and raucous laughter. They were a gang of regulars from the Mallorquina group (Lloréns, Canales, Muñoz Marín, the Dominican consul Sócrates Nolasco, and others) who had come down to have a little fun and entertain themselves at the expense of two patient and gullible fishermen."

Palés Matos was a recently arrived poet to San Juan. Diego Padró introduced him at a literary gathering in La Mallorquina. Founded in 1848, La Mallorquina was our Prendes or Café Tortoni, and it was the oldest restaurant in Puerto Rico. It was an auspicious literary debut for that naive youth from the town of Guayama who, with his muddied shoes, still carried something of the rustic into the grand literary world of San Juan. Diego Padró writes:

> On that night, as soon as they brought the order of coffee and toast to the table, Palés let a look fall across the porcelain plate they'd placed to the side accompanying the service. And then he smiled feebly at me and said in a hushed voice:
> "Chico, what a small portion of cheese they serve here!"
> I could barely contain myself. "That isn't cheese," I told him. "It's congealed butter."
> "Ah!" he exclaimed, and immediately took on the appearance of an ostrich, lowering his head and sinking his chin (damn near) in his cup of coffee, embarrassed, confused and blushing like a child for his mistake.

The group at La Mallorquina was made up of the most famous names in Puerto Rican letters from the first three decades of the twentieth century, nearly all gentlemen of excellent lineage and dressed to the hilt. Women were not allowed. We can imagine these names as well as those of an earlier generation (the generation of the rock-throwers) resounding in the new urban experience of Luis Palés Matos. From a small town in the south where he once asked God for mercy because nothing ever happened, the poet came to the city where his exceptional talent would have to guard against the easy flattery of the pretentious as well as the jealousies, suspicions, and bitterness of those who lacked his artistic genius.

But Diego Padró's dearest memory would have to be the "invitation to a voyage" hinted at by his fondness for the port and the wharf. The incitement to poetry as a cure for tropical weariness was always accompanied by an unredeemable nostalgia, a spiritual state Palés Matos would explore in his poems "Los animales interiores," "Voz de lo sendentario y lo monótono," and later "El Pozo." Then, at the height of the twenties, the port city held the promise of escape from the dull provincial life into a city where arrival was simply another means of departure. In his baroque and sensory-rich prose, Diego Padró describes for us the pier where they shared both the strength of their imagination and the weakness of a mad nostalgia:

> It was the small one, the white one situated between the Valdés Pier and the old customs and arsenal buildings. All that's left now is a dirty, gooey puddle with trash floating about in it. But, back then, it was filled with small vessels: Coast Guard ships, fishing boats, schooners and yachts for coastal traffic, all of which enlivened the air with the cries of their crews, the mix of tar and glue with the smell of both fresh and salted fish, of leather recently tanned, crates of fruits and vegetables from the country, patchouli, sugar, all the goods from their stuffed and overflowing holds. No decoration was more appropriate for opening an escape hatch to the interior torrent of our fantasies! There we were reciting poetry, discussing readings and smoking cigarettes until the calm, fresh hour when the cock crows and the horse brays for dawn.

The literary movement they established found its innocent and enthusiastic seed here. That pier was the site of a youthful passion.

This bohemian San Juan, the consecration of the old quarter as a space that inspired the imagination because it carried within it a legendary past, continued throughout the decades of the forties and fifties. In the working-class Bar Seda, located in the alley between Calle San Sebastián and Boulevard del Valle, in front of the entrance to La Perla (the place where terrified adolescents overdosing on crack let loose their screams), René Marqués, Pedro Juan Soto, Emilio Díaz Valcárcel, Tony Maldonado, and Rafael Tufiño, with bow ties now absent and sleeves rolled up, held gatherings for artists and writers from the Division of Community Education. That noble project, created by Luis Muñoz Marín, whose foundations were in a realism committed to educating the peasant masses, produced some of our most distinguished public mural art and literature committed to a social theme, one that bears witness to immigration, the move from the country to the city, and the bitter fruits of urban dispossession.

In the sixties, I met Don Tomás Blanco—already an old man— in the Colibrí Gallery, which at that time was located on the Callejón de la Capilla next to the famous Fonda del Callejón where in the second half of the sixties another gathering was born. That group was not quite so luminous as the groups in the Bar Seda or La Mallorquina, though they were equally inclined to banter. Father Bernard Kanfush, Frankie Cátala, Luis Muñoz Arjona, and Luiggi Marozzini, owner of the Colibrí Gallery, continued that San Juan tradition. The difference in this gathering from La Mallorquina or the Bar Seda had to do with the way they sat at the bar resting their feet on the edge and the manner in which they chugged their drinks, then slammed them on the counter. It was a small bar, with few stools, and the bartender, if memory serves me, was named Anselmo. He had a severe mustache like García Márquez, which did not distract from his demeanor as the perfect host. He was the first sententious bartender that I had met during my drinking period. Don Tomás Blanco, the author of *Prontuario Histórico* and *Los cinco sentidos,* sat in an armchair lording over the city and its political and literary history. He was a presence disposed to walk the streets in possession of both the visible setting of the urban landscape and the invisible one of history. At that time, the tract *Miserere* had been published, and his discussion of Rouault's painting seemed to me representative of a universalist ambition that was, at the same time, profoundly Puerto Rican.

During the sixties and seventies San Juan produced a bohemian life that replaced the restaurant with the café-theater as the gathering place. Café-theaters like La Tierruca, La Tea, La Tahona, and Las Tarolas appeared out of nowhere. It was a leftist and folkloric bohemianism, flavored with protest songs, the *nueva trova,* and South American music. David Ortiz and Pedro Zervigón recited Neruda and Nicolás Guillén while Sylvia Del Villard danced to the black poetry of Palés Matos and introduced an African style born of the Antilles yet not exempt from a certain hyperbolic exoticism. I took the huge billboard from La Tierruca and carted it to the bedroom of my adolescent daydreams, an odd prank from my distant youth that still leaves me perplexed today. I remember Miguel Ángel Suárez doing a dramatized reading in La Tea of the story *La noche que volvimos a ser gente* by José Luis González, who also happened to be present. La Tahona was founded by the poets Edwin Reyes and Antonio "El Topo" Cabán Vale, who waited tables at the same time that they were composing verses. Back then, El Topo composed the last national hymn that my generation offered to the Puerto Rican songbook: "Verde luz" exhibited a deep affinity with "Lamento Borincano" and "La Borinqueña." Las Tarolas, established in the same area in the seventies, was a powerful symbol of the independence movement in Old San Juan. They arrested Pedro Albizu Campos in the upper level of that building after the nationalist revolt in 1950 and again after the attack on the United States Congress in 1954. In Las Tarolas, Héctor "Atabal" Rodríguez and Radamés Sánchez wanted to create a café-theater with a movie projector that played classic films and offered free peanuts at each table. None of it worked; the place went under. It was there Glenn Monroig made his artistic debut.

Back then the Ocho Puertas was the chic "cabaret" par excellence. Situated on the corner of Calle Fortaleza con Cristo and in front of La Danza Restaurant, which is still open after four decades, Ocho Puertas, with its symbolic eight doors and closed lattice windows designed to create a "cozy" intimacy, was a sanctuary for the heart-breaking songs of Edith Piaf and the satirical cabaret of Rafi Muñoz. Eartha Kitt sang there in the closing stages of her career, and Liza Minnelli in the beginning of hers. Yvonne Coll premiered her Spanish "Un país tropical" in the same period she appeared in *Godfather II*. Ocho Puertas was the cocktail lounge where Joe Valiente played the piano and Danny Rivera and Lucecita Benítez gave encores. With its somewhat decadent décor (walls papered in violet tones with a suggestion of velvet in the ambience) and its gay owners (one gregarious, the other morose), Ocho Puertas was a symbol of the big city in a place that was still provincial. That cabaret dreamed of the decadence of other cities. Even though the guitar music of Tuti Umpierre would evoke the vanished singer and songwriter Sylvia Rexach in the voice of her daughter, Sharon Riley, in reality the nostalgia was not for the Berlin cabarets of the twenties and thirties but for the perverse Havana nightlife of the forties and fifties for which San Juan yearned. It was in Ocho Puertas where we discovered, in Carmen Delia Dipiní's voice and the boleros of Puchi Balseiro, that Cuban variant of the bolero that is the "feeling," a form halfway between cocktail lounge jazz and the sentimental ballad.

Recinto Sur, with its wharf, port, and pier, was not simply an unusual enticement for the "invitation to a voyage" that is literature. In José Curet's novel *Crimen en la Calle Tetuán* he paints the southern section for us as a place in which nineteenth-century city life teemed with gleams of mysterious initiations in entryways, behind lattice windows, and in tiny rooms where one could barely breathe, with the smell of onion and garlic knocking on the doors. The setting of that detective novel at the end of the nineteenth century, in a time where the mystery would be heightened by a still greater inscrutability, was a stroke of genius. In other words he set the novel in a past only seen through yellowed newspapers and lost folios—in the realm of the historian. In it, he describes for us Gámbaro Alley with its irregular design:

Some of these places have etched into their names a sound, which passes through the nervous system and into the protruding bone, showing us something of ourselves. The same thing occurs in the capital where I now live. It's like a drunken shrimp, like a stream of poorly placed flag stones, a diagonal design drawn without a chalk line or carpenter's square—dissecting parallels with Tetuán below, Fortaleza above, and, in the middle, Gámbaro.

The hills that rise above the north valley on the other side of the bay, which at times remind us of Lisbon or the Boca Grande of Cartagena de Indias, are of similar proportion and height. This karstic region would have seemed like an extraordinary Chinese landscape to the eighteenth- and nineteenth-century city before the construction of the Puerto Nuevo in the twentieth century and before the disorderly construction of the new Puerto Rico in the twenty-first century. That strange, surprising, and little-known landscape had to have been an invitation to dream because its symmetry and rhythm seem more a product of fantasy than reality, something nocturnal, though without the terror of a nightmare. The hills would be a peculiarity of the panorama seen from the city and an ominous incongruity for the invader.

The Puntilla-Marina sector in the lower part of the city also dreamed of a Europe around the end of the nineteenth century. The Paseo de La Princesa is a reconstruction of the Paseo de La Puntilla, which had already been planned by the second half of that century. Conceived according to the bourgeois aspirations of the Madrid boulevards, which in turn were modeled on the Parisian boulevards and made possible by the destruction of the walls, it was an accomplishment like that of the imperial Spanish bastion over the islet of San Juan. However, the boulevard served as yet another sign of the future of a city dedicated to the commerce of its citizens rather than the defense of Spain's last American possession. La Puntilla sector, where Palés Matos and Diego Padró went fishing in the twenties, was converted, back in the second half of the nineteenth century, into a neighborhood containing both warehouses and residential housing. It represented an expansion of the city and a symbol of its commercial future. The destruction of the neighborhood in the 1960s signified the loss of a city outside the walls that testified to a new era. It was a violation of its recent past. With the loss of La Puntilla and the destruction of the old train station between the walled city and the Paseo de Covadonga—the route to the Puerta de Tierra neighborhood—part of the city's history vanished into the ether. No longer an evocation of the city's textured life, the neighborhood was relegated to a depository of facts for the urban historian.

8

La Puerta de Tierra

At the end of the nineteenth century, it was the neighborhood of maids and servants, of the proletariat that sustained the bourgeois aspirations of the old city. Its growth made possible the creation of new types of living quarters, such as the tenement houses already common in many old quarters across the Caribbean. These houses existed halfway between miserable overcrowding and Fourier's communal utopia. Puerta de Tierra contains these proletarian memories as well as those inherent in a port city: the houses of prostitution, the nightclubs with their lascivious dancing, the dives like that of the Italian American Tursi, where my generation had its sexual initiation, moving from the whores' cynicism to their glazed and fiery eyes, their sexuality abated only with the promise of tobacco. Today the possibilities of the secret wharf remain; it is full of cheap diners and bars, like La Coal's fishermen's co-op behind Crowley's dock, with cheap beer and yellow perch fried in lard. Sammy, the owner of La Coal, will remember many years later how that neighborhood was rescued from the mud in the bay while Múcaro Thurman's foul balls resounded through the Sixto Escobar Park.

Further down we find the notorious El Falansterio. Designed in the thirties by the architect Jorge Ramírez de Arellano, its molding and Art Deco cornices, along with a style taken from the industrial towns and dreamed up by the French architect Tony Garnier, represented the first public housing project, a model that was discontinued in the designs of the new residences and urbanizations of the fifties. El Falansterio evokes memories of the tenement houses for which Puerta de Tierra was known. Its architecture restored something of a neighborhood on the crowded poor in the same way that it would also help to alleviate some of the misfortunes of the working-class world.

Puerta de Tierra has always been working class and artisan. In the thirties, Rafael Tufiño became an apprentice in Juan Rosado's art studio in Puerta de Tierra. On top of making designs for Carnival floats, Juan Rosado made publicity signs in his Art Sign Shop. In addition to this job, Juan Rosado achieved great artistic heights. His canvases entitled *La Espera* and *Desesperación* underlined his vision of art as a social document at the same time that they situated Puerto Rican painting (that sky seen from the balcony in *La Espera!*) in the specific, creamy light—a northern light—of that working-class neighborhood. There are long-suffering women who wait, like the women in Tufiño's *Allende los mares,* but without the consolation of a baby. There is machismo suggested in these paintings, the presence of a certain self-denial in the suffering of the woman who waits—for whom, we do not know. We can fantasize that is it a man from a superior social class. The women wear long dresses clinging to their figures, passing between the government offices and the evening bars. In any case, these are urban women, not women of the street. There is a certain *hembrismo* suggested by their poses, seemingly patient at first glance, for, like their neighborhood, they are women in a difficult transition between hope and the despair of knowing they are trapped.

In 1940 L'Atelier was founded in Puerta de Tierra, a center of art, music, and bohemianism dedicated to the cultivation of young painters, a group of whom included Tony Maldonado, Juan A. Rosado Jr., Rafael Tufiño, Luis Burgos, and Luis García. The musicians included Kachiro, Guillermo, and Rafael Figueroa. L'Atelier promoted culture in this addition to the old quarter until 1946.

Puerta de Tierra has that unique flavor of a place that, at some level, has remained at the edge of urban change. Its profile from the twenties, thirties, and forties withstood the greed of the developers and yuppies. At any rate, its gentrification has not yet occurred. It remains a place crowded with pool halls, bars, nightclubs, and discotheques that alternate between salsa on Fridays and reggaeton on Saturdays, a neighborhood filled with alleyways peopled with the dispossessed and adolescent addicts, aficionados of the high-grade marijuana known as "cripy" and the "Phillies" cigars stuffed with cocaine and weed, the notorious "little devils," all manifestations of a place as free with drugs as it is old in communal life. Not every corner, though, is a place of drugs. Some simply exemplify the old Puerto Rican vocation for dancing and hanging out.

In the section of Avenida Ponce de León that passes in front of Puerta de Tierra stands the San Agustín Parish, whose small bells inside the somewhat Byzantine oblong towers adorned with oxen eyes appear as if they were taken from a half-oriental, half-Mediterranean atmosphere. Here, the light from the city is exotic. The salty marine air climbs the tower as if searching for some definition of its foreign nature, proof that architecture is also a meeting place for diverse environments, for distant cities with similar brilliance.

On the other side of Puerta de Tierra, toward the south, there is a little tongue of land that sticks out into the bay that used to be known as Miraflores. The site of skirmishes and battles during the English attack of 1797, it is a place of deep darkness in *El camino de Yyaloide,* where canals lead to the lagoons east of the city, first the Martín Peña or San José Lagoons and later Cangrejos. There, a young Niño Avilés would search for the metaphor of that other city, the lacustrine site of erotic enchantment and incestuous acts, the route of the Arcadian city and the reshaped romantic novel.

Miraflores was converted into Isla Grande at the end of the twenties when they filled it with rock taken from the hills in Cantera along the route that follows the canal toward the San José Lagoon.

The Isla Grande Airport was built in Miraflores, constructed during the bellicose spirit of World War II and on the site where a large part of the resident agricultural workers, known as "tomateros" during the forties and fifties, embarked for the North. It was there I would both welcome and say good-bye to my father on his visits to the States as a government official. And it was in that melancholic airport, which I remember as an enormous hangar, that V. S. Naipaul, in his autobiographical novel *The Enigma of Arrival,* set his passage from Trinidad and the Caribbean to England, the country that would eventually announce his arrival to the world. In the airport scene, Naipaul focuses on a black traveler who will become his reflection and upon whom he will reflect throughout that voyage to the unknown. His somewhat obsessive attention to this character reaches such a height of fascination that the surrounding Isla Grande Airport blurs into the background of his chronicle. The people grow silent; the voices of the *jíbaros* (peasants) about to board the Pan Am Clipper are scarcely heard. The writer mentions them, but only in passing. The details of both the place and its significance are obliterated, a good example of the author's Caribbean neurasthenia and solipsism.

The Luis Muñoz Rivera Park culminates in a secret, Art Deco city consisting mostly of government buildings, almost all of which are associated with the naval and army bases standing as a silent, colonial inheritance of World War II. We arrive now on the south side of Muñoz Rivera Park, a place Múcaro Thurman's foul balls never reached. We are in an area of low trees, where the layout of the avenues culminates in roundabouts, and where the Art Nouveau style of the benches lining the paths imitates the trunks and branches of the symmetric little forest, all suggestive of a fairy tale. The north side of Muñoz Rivera Park looks to the sea and to the cliff beside bus stop 8 where the balls hit by Josh Gibson and Frank Howard did reach; and it is here where the tall Australian Pines sway in the ocean breeze.

There, in the square between Sixto Escobar Park and the Caribe Hilton Hotel, we find the Normandie Hotel. It was designed by the architect Raúl Reichard and built by Félix Benítez Rexach—the Puerto Rican engineer and bon vivant who made his fortune in the service of Rafael Leonidas Trujillo—following the model of a visionary and capricious naval architecture with Caribbean characteristics, because boat-like designs also flourished in the mansions of Santo Domingo. In the kitschy style of a provincial engineer who dreamed of travel and a place in the wide world, he conceived of the façade of his hotel as an imitation of the Normandie ocean liner. The design has Art Deco influences but without the cliché of grooved molding. It resembles the bridge of a visionary boat stranded in the bend between the Sixto Escobar Park and the entrance to the Caribe Hilton. The Normandie Hotel is acknowledged in the architecture of the recently constructed Millennium condominiums, located on the far east side of Muñoz Rivera Park. It is one of the few examples, in this eclectic, discordant city, of a building that in its decline dreamed up another nearby building, this time arrogant about its privileged location in front of the Condado lagoon, the sea, and the bay. In San Juan the urban landscape is almost always taken hostage by the power of money. Here, postmodern architecture places the Art Deco of the Normandie between the noise of mega-dollars and bad urban planning. The Millennium condominium complex, with its privileged view over three different bodies of water, privatizes an exceptional landscape of our urban fabric.

9

A Clear Space,
a Vigil for Poets

The San Antonio Bridge connected Miraflores with the so-called island because Puerto Ricans use the word "island" to mean the "interior" of the country, like when we say, "Voy para la isla!" (I'm going to the island!). The implicit meaning is that of the old settlement on the islet of San Juan and how this islet is separate from the "big island"—i.e., the rest of Puerto Rico. San Juan Bautista was an islet connected by a bridge and susceptible to being cut off as it could easily be surrounded, making the San Antonio Bridge and surrounding Miraflores of extreme strategic importance during the English attack of 1797.

This confluence of bridges and crossroads between the "big island" and the islet of San Juan has often been photographed. It appears and reappears in postcards dating from the beginning of the twentieth century. In one postcard the San Antonio Bridge appears to have been photographed from the east side. Standing out over the pillars, the light posts shine with a light that seems less fake than it does today. In another postcard, dating from 1909 and taken from the Miramar side, the bridge appears older still. The pillars that mark the ends are not visible, and the railings, forming a grill of crisscrossed steel, present a fitting legacy from an age enamored with iron. In the foreground we observe a bucolic scene, children playing

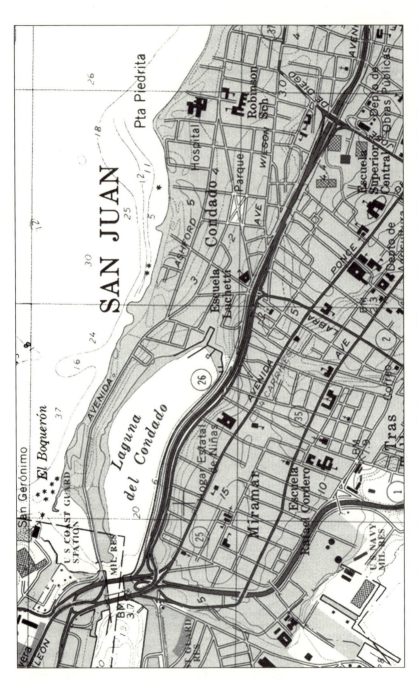

Condado sits east of the islet of San Juan (connected by the San Antonio Bridge) and just north of Santurce. The Dos Hermanos Bridge is not labeled on the map but connects the north shore of the Condado Lagoon with the islet of Old San Juan at the point that is labeled "U.S. Coast Guard Station" on the map.

between the bushes, coco plums, and mangroves that reach to the lagoon. In the distance we catch a glimpse of the San Gerónimo Fort with its unusual raised-wood construction covering the battlements like some kind of patch.

In other postcards we see San Gerónimo from the eastern shore of Miraflores near the mouth of the San Antonio Canal, a panoramic view from the military road that used to cross the bridge on its way toward Miramar, Santurce, Hato Rey, and finally Río Piedras. Filled with palms, the place always fought to remain spacious, though today they are planning to build an enormous urban center with malls, apartments, restaurants, and parking lots. In other words, in place of the ocean breeze, the light, the palms, and the splendid views in the postcard there will be a concrete jungle. The coastline has been eroded almost to the point that the lower section has been lost. On the postcard the coastline is almost flush against the ocean, a place for coco plums and palms, which used to be on the outskirts, on the edges of the islet. In another postcard of the San Gerónimo Fort, taken from the gardens of the Caribe Hilton Hotel, one gets a detailed view of the wooden edifice of the fort, a sort of pavilion or barracks constructed over the battlements, ramps, and patios. It is as if this bastion of defense for the east flank of San Juan were more a curiosity, an exercise in eccentricity, as much then as it is now. Is it a sacrilege of the Yankee Empire with respect to the Spanish, or, the contrary: an architectural irreverence from an empire in its decline?

The other bridge, called Dos Hermanos, was a late addition to our history, built toward the end of the nineteenth and the beginning of the twentieth centuries. Perhaps it was built out of the need to finally connect the islet of San Juan with the lower parts of Cangrejos, with those noxious and poisonous lagoons where runaway black slaves, as well as fugitives from other islands, gathered in a sort of sanctuary during the Spanish rule. The privateer, Miguel Enríquez, controlled Cangrejos, with property under his rule seen as a gift from the protectorate and viewed approvingly by the Spanish

Crown. While the San Antonio Bridge connected the islet with the "King's Highway" to Río Piedras, along the high ridge of Cangrejos where Santurce is today, the Dos Hermanos Bridge communicated with secret places, sunken lands, and hidden palm groves. From there the Condado neighborhood includes in its recent history—as opposed to that of the nineteenth century—the paradox of being, like Miramar, a place privileged with a view of the Atlantic while at the same time having been marginalized, almost forgotten.

In another postcard we glimpse, in the landscape concealed by coco palms, the place where the Condado Plaza Hotel would be built in the sixties. It is an idyllic space that remains faithful to the text of this particular postcard written in 1947. The writer notes that in spite of the few people who speak English (Puerto Rico being a North American Possession!), the land is a paradise. This person, whose voice today sounds like that of a ghost, praises the ocean view from his room in the Condado Vanderbilt Hotel. Today Condado's public beaches sit on the north side of the lagoon. We guess that's the place because in the photo we recognize the mound to the far left where we now find the pool gardens. The picture has been taken from the Dos Hermanos Bridge, and in the left corner we can also discern San Gerónimo's legendary "dog," a rock in a canine shape.

Taking in the panoramic sweep of this confluence of roads, bridges, and history, the city hesitates in the face of its own metaphor because it is the place where the Condado Lagoon encounters the wild Atlantic. The urban landscape opts for the coastal gaze stretching to the horizon rather than the more introspective look toward the lagoon with its jagged cut of mangroves, palms, marshes, plains, and hills.

This amalgamation is our urban star, our *étoile,* the site of a magical, metaphorical convergence that confers drama to the city. It is exactly that privileged space cited in so many postcards. It represents a found place, a place of meetings, of communal gatherings, all fragments of the fabric or of the urban "text." The postcard extracts a part of the urban fabric and converts it into a symbolic fragment that represents a familiar space for the inhabitants of the city and an astonishing site for its visitors.

The postcards were made from linen paper with watercolors applied over the print, a process that lasted until the forties. This method conferred upon the urban landscape the benefit of a double purpose: the photography took the place out of the urban fabric and converted it into an eloquent fragment of the city, while the color was the photographic equivalent of sepia, evoking memory, adding age to that which is too familiar, too present.

There is, in the postcards, a poetics of the city. When the city is painted in these cards, it becomes picturesque, pictorial, acquiring an interpretive gaze that is, in itself, melancholic, yearning. More than anything, those postcards reveal the solitude of the urban landscape. The human figure becomes the transgressor. We search for the city as interpreter, the protagonist of its own drama. It is the city as a character type, or, in other words, a flat persona yet with the hint of a depth that exists beyond the photographic "click."

This instantaneous veil of nostalgia and exoticism transforms the city into a place of dreams, a place to be dreamed. I see the postcard of Los Angeles in the thirties and I recall the "noir" Los Angeles of Raymond Chandler's novels and those postmodern references made by the contemporary novelist James Ellroy. It is the symbolic postcard that reveals a crossroads: the façade of the NBC Radio Center, Los Angeles's "Radio City" in the Sunset Boulevard neighborhood. Not a single human is present. Los Angeles is the city of the automobile; two thirds of its terrain is dedicated to parking lots. On the other side of Sunset Boulevard, one Art Deco building follows another, illuminated by the glow of nightclubs and restaurants like Tropics and The Brown Derby. The automobiles are from the thirties and forties; the street lamps hanging over the desolate sidewalks glow with a yellow, spectral light. There is a traffic jam, but I do not see the people. On the other side of the Art Deco NBC Building, we see a Sunset Boulevard that is even more forlorn, so much so it is almost alarming. The full moon shines through the dark clouds, an ominous sign, which Philip Marlowe, driving in a Packard in *The Little Sister,* passing along the succession of Art Deco façades, describes along with the rest of the urban landscape he knew so well.

What are the definitive signs of this postal landscape, which we recognize in the entrance to the Condado neighborhood? The city is flat here, scarcely disturbed by the profile of the Caribe Hilton sitting in harmony with the topography of the coastline. On the other side of the Dos Hermanos Bridge, the landscape hardly changes in both the Hotel Condado Plaza and its beach, which continues to the far east end of the bridge. Here the city takes on an ambience unlike any other place. There are no towers to alter this horizontal scene, accentuated in the area where Avenida Baldorioty borders the Condado Lagoon. San Gerónimo Fort with its low battlements and buttresses also highlights the horizontality of the Caribe Hilton before the construction of its tower annex. Even with these buildings interrupting the view, the city's desire for an unobstructed skyline remains, its need to exist as a city without the tunnel effect of narrow streets running, like canyons, between the tall buildings. The entrance to the Condado neighborhood emphasizes a city open to the tropical, Caribbean light.

In the fictional neighborhood of Alamares, a name created by the writer Rosario Ferré for the ambience of her novel *La casa de la laguna,* we can visualize the two metaphors that compete at this crossroads in the city:

> Alamares occupied a narrow strip of land, crossed from one end to the other by Avenida Ponce de León and had, as we say, two faces. One of them, the most public, faced north toward the Atlantic Ocean and a beautiful beach of white sand. The most private and tranquil faced south toward the Alamares lagoon and had no beach. By the side of the lagoon, the avenue ran into a mangrove swamp that seemed to have no beginning.

However, it is the lagoon we today call Condado that inspired the construction of the legendary house: "The lagoon was clear and deep and, towards dusk, its reflection hung, like an aquamarine of several carats, from the slender neck of the Puente del Agua."

The house reaches its greatest definition when the architect Pavel, a character inspired by Nechodoma, designed the terrace: "Finally, behind the house, Pavel designed his tour de force: a terrace made of golden mosaics that projected boldly over the lagoon. In that place, Rebeca would be able to hold gatherings with her artist friends."

Ferré tells us how these houses for the newly rich carried an unusual curse, one that isolated their inhabitants from the rest of the city, given the "purified paradise" in which they were constructed: "The rumor about the houses designed by Pavel was that they exercised a malevolent influence over their inhabitants, causing them to lose their minds. For example, the Behn brothers, known throughout San Juan as 'los Hermanos Brothers,' owners of the telephone company, were so content in their beautiful mansion at the entrance to Alamares that they never came out."

Perhaps it was this sort of indecision between the lagoon and the ocean, a provincial echo of the great Venetian lagoon and the Lido overlooking the Adriatic, that fascinated the architect who designed the Condado Vanderbilt Hotel in the twenties. The entrance of the hotel looked out to the lagoon, while the guests had a view of the beautiful and rugged Atlantic Ocean.

The oscillation between the two metaphors is evident in the postcards of the Condado Vanderbilt. In one, taken from the east bank of the Condado Lagoon where the promenade that borders Avenida Baldorioty de Castro ends today, we can see the imposing building of the hotel in the wasteland of what Condado once was. The entire place is devoid of coconut palms, as if it had been cut down and cleared to make room for other buildings. The sea lies behind the hotel, the lagoon in front. In a picture that is not an aerial view, one taken from the same east bank but flush with the water, this "hotel by the lagoon" appears surrounded by vegetation: pines, shrubs, and mangroves. In the back, to the left, one recognizes the

Dos Hermanos Bridge. The picture must have been taken after the picture of the wasteland. In a third postcard, taken from the same place, we can see the sumptuous hotel framed by coco palms and clumps of banana trees backed by a coastal panorama not that different from the countryside. The back of the hotel is obscured by a pine grove on the north bank of the lagoon.

In the mid-fifties the architect Miguel Ferrer—who in 1949 had already designed the Caribe Hilton Hotel with its gracious horizontal lines in search of the coastline and its invisible presence never disturbing the area's beauty—opted for the ocean as a metaphor for Condado and the city. The La Concha Hotel, located in the section of Condado without a view of the lagoon and constructed during the development and tourism furor of the fifties, revealed a middle elevation, situated harmoniously within the surrounding urban landscape as well as the startling marine scenery of Ferré's fictional Alamares. But there was something disturbing about the hotel's location because it was built almost on the beach in a manner that denied the city the use of a marine boulevard. The shell-shaped building that was built to accommodate the nightclub would become emblematic of the tropical mentality of that time while simultaneously hinting at the predatory instinct of the city, that of viewing its marine landscape as a place for entertainment. It marked the beginning of the privatization of the marine landscape and its preservation, not as a place for contemplation of the scenery, as had been done in other cities from Havana to Río de Janeiro, but rather for the entertainment of tourists, sun worshippers, and swimmers. It would become the blueprint for the future development of the hotel and tourist industry to the east, culminating in Isla Verde's excess, which resulted in a proliferation of condominiums as the protagonists of this de facto privatization of the beach. It is interesting that the tourist development was carried out in one of the most dangerous beaches in San Juan with its strong currents and permanent undertow.

It is not without irony that the Spanish poet Pedro Salinas wrote one of the great sea poems of the twentieth century while living in

Condado during the second half of the forties. His insistence on contemplating the ocean, on viewing it as an object of contemplation, should have opened up a public debate for a government that in those years was more educated than any we have had.

In the dedication to the collection of poems entitled *El Contemplado,* published in 1946, he places the inescapable point of his inspiration there, in the ocean vista of San Juan:

> To the Afda brotherhood,
> in whose generous hospitality
> these poems were conceived.
> The ocean of Puerto Rico
> 1943–1944

In "El Contemplado," the poem that establishes the marine theme of the book, the poet tells us:

> From gazing at you so long,
> from the horizon to the sand,
> slowly,
> from the snail to the colored sky,
> brilliance upon brilliance, wonder upon wonder
> I have named you; the eyes
> found it, watching you.
> . . . .
> You have been for me,
> from the day
> when my eyes opened to you,
> the contemplated, the forever
> Contemplated!

In his letters Salinas seems to especially treasure the experience of looking out over the ocean from Condado. He writes to Juan Centeno, speaking of his daily routine: "I haven't stopped enjoying the outside air for a single day, reading beside the sea, or working in the terrace of the Afda Club, which is my office." With great specificity, he notes the short distance between the terrace of the Afda Club, where he wrote *El Contemplado,* to the open air, the *plein air,* and the beach:

I can't see the ocean from our house, though I can hear it at night because it's near, perhaps two hundred meters. So, I go like a drunk to the corner tavern two or three times a day to catch a glimpse of the ocean, to drink it with my eyes. Alone and happy. San Juan is enchanting. The old quarter reminds one of a small city in Andalusia or Levante, full of life, of noise, and filled with homes like in Almería or Huelva.

The universal Spaniard compares San Juan with similar cities in the Spanish peninsula. It is his discovery, as well as ours, of a shared legacy, that of light, of the diaphanous Mediterranean and Andalusian radiance. Later, he insists on the idolatry of our sea:

> I idolize the sea. Each day, I spend many hours on the club terrace, which is very near to the house and which serves as an excellent vantage point. I take my books there and work in the outside air in perfect peace and in a temperature that is always mild. My time at the club is so regular that I jokingly call the terrace where I work my "office." I have just finished a long poem and am now writing another in various parts on an ocean theme.

In these verses, he discovers for us the blue of our Atlantic:

> Variations that were taught
> in school: Aegean, Atlantic,
> Indian, Caribbean, Marmara,
> Sea of the Sunda, the White Sea.
> All are one to my eyes:
> the blue of the Contemplated.
> . . . .
> Each time I went looking for you,
> I found you there, in your glory,
> you who have never failed me.
> Your blueness explains itself:
> blue color, paradise;
> and looking at you, I see it.

Later he reminds us what it is to be an island searching for its meaning while gazing on its own shores:

Brief, happy dream. The last
marvel yet remains to be discovered:
it is the seashore.
The islands stop, amazed,
upon arriving at the edge of life.

Salinas shows us how the gaze that stretches over the marine horizon, the eye that searches for light, triumphs over death:

This desire to see is more than mine.
One feels the silent, alien push,
rising from the ancient darkness,
revealing itself to those
eyes with which I gaze. The endless dead
that have looked upon you
ask for my gaze, to see you again!

To deny ourselves light is to embark on the walk toward death. And I ask myself about this insistence on light. I suppose that it has something to do with my age and that of Don Pedro Salinas because it is only at our age that one discovers a certain intimacy with time. If it is true that I am in the infancy of old age, the same age in which Salinas wrote *El Contemplado,* then we are at the stage when that ancient and strange idea of fleeing from ourselves assaults us. It is like escaping, there, in the surrender to light, the inevitability of time. Melancholy lies in wait in our escape toward the light; darkness creeps toward us.

I stumble upon a picture taken of Pedro Salinas around 1946, the year *El Contemplado* was published, and the year I was born. He is dressed in white linen and about the same age as I am now. And I tell myself that this is the image of a poet hanging onto a salvation found in the blinding, tropical light of the Caribbean.

However, my salvation would come down to chance. I finally cured myself of my hermetic vocation. It happened in the seventies, when I stopped contemplating the sea and began swimming in it instead near the long Alambique beach. I discovered the light stretching out over our city, which, in spite of the eccentric buildings and condominiums, still maintains its presence over the length of the coastline. It is the same light that Salinas, that cultivator of atmospheres, discovered when he visited Los Angeles for the first time. Salinas also read Chandler, though I do not know if that dazzling light owed more to Rafael Alberti than to the writer par excellence of the noir novel. At any rate, Pedro Salinas was a man who yearned for that clear luminosity of cities evocative of the Mediterranean. He wrote to Jorge Guillén:

> California, and above all Los Angeles, has seduced me through the pure grace of its light and its urban originality. One of my manias is collecting cities, and among them, Los Angeles is one of the premiere examples. It has an air of temporality, of a momentary city, having renounced any pretension of eternity or definitiveness, which makes it astonishing to wake up each morning to the fact that the city is still there. And it is the most luxurious in its use of space of all the cities I know. Horizontal light isn't channeled through the tall avenues, but spills out over everything, lasting longer than in other cities.

Salinas's characterization of Los Angeles contains some of the definitive traits of San Juan, most important of which is the clear and luminous quality of the atmosphere over a city whose elevation is in harmony with the horizon, the coastline, and the lagoons.

I have asked myself many times: why the neurosis, why the old blindness for this light that surrounds me? I suppose that it was because I grew up in a village in the interior of the island, surrounded by mountains and hills, their smooth valleys sown with cane. It was a sea of green with a creamy light, not dazzling but with an intense glare, a light essentially different from that contemplated on the coastline. The clouds were always low and the light slipped into something that subjugated it, that conquered it. There the lack, which would later be desire, took root. The light of the coastline was, for me, a conquest, as I suppose it was for Salinas, who, born in Madrid so far from the sea, would have seen his horizon in silhouette, though in his case, the gaze would stumble toward the infinite ochre of the Castilian plateau.

El Contemplado was translated into English as *Sea of San Juan,* a title that reduces the poetry in the book while at the same time extolling the place of its inspiration. In the cover photograph, which we suppose shows the window of the bookstore where *Sea of San Juan* was sold, the book appears as the "First English Translation by Eleanor L. Turnbull of Baltimore from the book of poems by Dr. Pedro Salinas of the Johns Hopkins University." It is curious that part of its publicity would include picturesque photographs of our sea and coastline, as if the metaphysical vision of our sea that Salinas held dear was incapable of escaping the tourists' stranglehold.

Another great poet, the Caribbean writer and winner of the Nobel Prize for Literature, Derek Walcott, also walked the streets of Condado, carried away with the beauty of the "Sea of San Juan." His vision is more intimate and evocative, less metaphysical than that of Salinas. It is not stimulated by that expansion of the gaze unfolding toward the horizon of light, but rather by the discovery of epiphanic places scarcely seen from streets like Cervantes, which runs down to the beach. In "Tropic Zone I" he tells us of his habit of walking, attentive to that which we recognize as our own:

> This is my ocean, but it is speaking
> another language, since its accent changes around
> different islands. The wind is up early, campaigning
> with the leaflets of seagulls, but from the balcony
> of the guesthouse, I resist the return
> of this brightening noun whose lines must be translated
> into "el mar" or "la mar," and death itself to "la muerte."

Later, the location of Condado becomes clear:

> Changed to a light shirt, I walk out to Cervantes Street.
> Shadow-barred. A water sprinkler or a tank approaches.
> The corners are empty. The boulevards open like novels
> waiting to be written. Clouds like the beginnings of stories.

As so often happens in Walcott, the poetic ecstasy is a meditation over ancestral memory, over the many things that have happened in these lands, which had once seen genocide:

> Along white-walled, palm-splashed Condado, the breeze smells
> of a dialect so strong it is not disinfected
> by the exhausts of limousines idling outside the hotels,
> while, far out, unheard, the grinding reef of the Morro
> spits out like corals the indigestible sorrow
> of the Indian, bits for the National Museum.

Here the clear nature of the San Juan landscape hides the sin of Cain, bound by the unnamable crime. Suddenly the epiphany, the revelation that inspires the walk, turns dramatic:

> Blue skies convert all genocide into fiction,
> but a man, drawn to the seawall, crouches like a question
> or a prayer, and my own prayer is to write
> lives as mindless as the ocean's of linear time,
> since time is the first province of Caesar's jurisdiction.

Walcott's Condado penetrates the architecture and the symbols of an oppressive, colonial past. It emphasizes the preponderance of the "international" tourist architecture and points out the vulnerability of a society that attempts to glorify a past built on humiliation and exploitation. If Pedro Salinas's gaze toward the horizon and the temple of the sea is contemplative, Walcott's is a testimony to the history of the Caribbean. He concludes the third part of "Tropic Zone" by making an allusion to a beer advertisement heard as he stares at the wall mural of a luxurious hotel. While the beer is eulogized, his satire on the rhetoric of the mural turns sarcastic. The Indians represented there, the inhabitants of Eden, look on with the catatonic faces of those who have suffered through history:

> Above hot tin billboards, above Hostería del Mar,
> wherever the Empire has raised the standard of living
> by blinding high rises, gestures are made to the culture
> of a remorseful past, whose artists must stay unforgiving
> even when commissioned. If the white architectural mode is

International Modern, the décor must be the Creole's,
so, in a terra-cotta lobby with palms, a local jingle
gurgles of a new cerveza, frost-crusted and golden,
right next to a mural that has nationalized Eden.
. . . .
Then, shy as the ferns their hands are bending, stare
fig-nippled maidens with faces calm as stones,
and, as is the case with so many revolutions,
the visitor doubts the murals and trusts the beer.

10

From Borinquen Park
It Is One Step
to Villa Palmeras

However, Condado is not just a place for poets to roam amidst buildings with an Art Deco flair to more traditional structures lacking imagination; it is also a site of generic, "international" architecture that doesn't quite resemble Miami, much less itself. Out of all the neighborhoods in the city, it is the one most identified with riches and economic power. On the corner of Calle de Diego and Avenida Ashford, just before arriving at "Indio Park," which used to be called Borinquen Park, we are surprised by the ostentation that comes from money. You might even say that on that corner and in the surrounding condominiums you will find the richest place in the Caribbean. It might be an ethnocentric boast, but what is certain is that the fierce positioning of the tall condominiums hides any view of the sea, sequestering it for the private use of the rich and making manifest the conjunction of the arrogance of the privileged classes with an urban planning, which has characterized the development of a San Juan coastline that is centered upon the needs of the wealthy classes. According to the laws of the Commonwealth of Puerto Rico, all the beaches are public and everyone should be permitted to access them. So, why not an ocean view?

In this shady corner of flower shops and boutiques, of chic restaurants with French pretensions, or a delicatessen selling caviar and

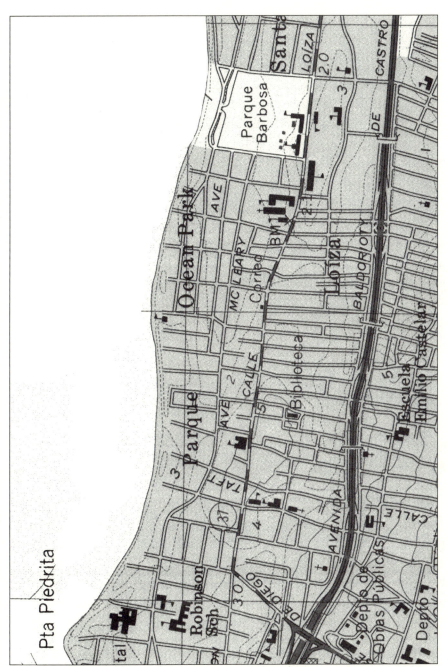

Ocean Park, a middle-class and rather affluent neighborhood. Borinquen Park, or what is now known as Indio Park, lies just to the west.

foie gras, the next neighborhood begins to insinuate itself. Its name, Ocean Park, evokes Parque Borinquen, or Borinquen Park, always translated to the foreign tongue or given a temporary nickname because it is now known as Indio Park—referring to the Taíno Indians, according to the statue that adorns the park. The adjoining neighborhood is known as Terraza del Parque. The last trolley line used to end in Ocean Park, which gives us a glimpse into its almost suburban character around the beginning of the twentieth century. It was a neighborhood where the coastline was filled with coconut palms, and the view of the Atlantic Ocean was expansive.

On the right-hand side, toward the high end of Calle de Diego, the Casa Vieja Restaurant sits alongside the Shell station on the corner of Calle Loíza. Dating from the twenties and thirties, Casa Vieja was a somewhat rundown wooden building with a balcony around the circumference, a humble yet distinguished mansion discarded by the surrounding development. In Casa Vieja, we celebrated the publication of *La noche oscura del Niño Avilés* after its presentation in the nearby bookstore Bell, Book & Candle.

In that presentation in 1984, José Luis González assured the public that never had a Puerto Rican novel gone so far in its use of imagination, a doubtful observation given my intuition that José Luis had not read further than the first chapter. Afterwards we gathered in the Casa Vieja, and, in a photo in front of the tapestry that covered the back wall of the dining room, I appear at thirty-eight years old together with a group of celebrities all of whom seemed to share the same sense of questioning. José Luis stands on the far right, his face cut off by the enthusiasm of the photographer. He is smiling and somewhat euphoric, his head, as always, tilted. Beside him is Catalino "Tite" Curet Alonso, lost in his own world, and in those years named "National Poet" by José Luis. He is wearing one of those "dashikis," which today are only worn by Ángel Quintero Rivera. Next to Catalino stands the singer Ismael Rivera, and between him and me, Orvil Miller, who was the true host of that party. There I am, about to drink more whiskey than I should, more watered-down

106

whiskey, which according to Saint Augustine is the most inebriating. I look stout, my shirt busting at the seams, and the tie without a jacket illuminates the fatality of middle age, the age of adultery, which was catching up with me. I am swollen, on the verge of consulting a liver doctor. Even though I doubted the words of José Luis in his presentation, I still considered myself called to literary greatness. One can see in me that strained innocence, which was an improvement over the surprise of finding myself in the middle of *Vea* magazine. But the focus of that photo is Ismael Rivera, who did not say a word throughout the night because of the polyps on his vocal chords and who probably wondered why the hell he was there at all. To complete the photo, we have the poet Jorge María Ruscalleda Bercedoniz and Cheo Feliciano, one of my all-time Puerto Rican favorites. In the picture, Feliciano still appears young, not so far removed from the hard times when he would sing with Joe Cuba. The lawyer Marcos Rivera is seated in front of Feliciano on the opposite side of Catalino.

For me, Casa Vieja remains a place of unlikely encounters because, during a good part of the late eighties, we formed a literary gathering on the terrace of the restaurant, including most notably Olga Nolla, Dr. Manuel Martínez Maldonado (poet, novelist, and world famous nephrologist), as well as the poets Hjalmar Flax and José Luis Vega. Occasionally we were visited by the architect and painter Nick Quijano, the philosopher Don José Echeverría, the literary critic and peninsular poet Carlos Bousoño, and José Luis González, who in 1989 would be in denial with respect to the fall of socialism, telling us that it was a momentary crisis of the Soviet system. Manolo Pavía, *flâneur* par excellence from the Terraza del Parque, also stopped in.

In a display of overt womanhood and habitual flirtatiousness, Olga made herself queen, wined and dined by the men in the group. If the gathering in the Mallorquina five decades before did not admit women, this gathering in Casa Vieja was governed and lightened by the beautiful smile of Olga, who loved the rice with squid that they served there, and who always proceeded to baptize it with a generous quantity of lemon. She was our empress, someone who knew how to placate the competition of egos battling for literary glory. It was, perhaps, Olga who went the farthest in that battle for glory with her tender and modest *corazón mayagüezano* (heart from Mayagüez), because, like a good cook, she always stretched the boundaries of her literary office, trying out new recipes instead of following old ones, relying on spontaneity and pride to achieve exquisite flavors without demeaning those of other writers. While Olga cheered us, the melancholic men who did not go to Vietnam, the white boys with fancy last names from the Terraza del Parque cartel, carried out their illegal deals in the back of the bar. That was another crazy encounter, which was the most famous "dish" of this place that lay somewhere between secrecy and pubic office. I mean public office!

Borinquen Park was, in 1909, a beautiful park in the middle of a forest of coconut palms. Here and there, gazebos dotted the landscape. But it was the palm fronds blowing in the breeze that caught the eye. The gazebos were made of wood, some crowned with roofs forming striking pinnacles, others with four-sided roofs. The benches sat under the frenzy of palm fronds, waiting for tired park visitors to sit and contemplate the sea. In this part of the park the sidewalk is wide and the view to the sea unobstructed. In one postcard, men wearing straw hats and overcoats and carrying umbrellas appear as if taken from a painting by Renoir and moved to the Caribbean. It would be our Belle Epoque! Puerto Rico seems to be a country in control of its destiny; ironically, we were living under the recently instated North American military regime. On the side of the sidewalk sloping down to the ocean, which in this postcard appears perfectly calm, without the surges and swells characteristic of that coastline, one can see several small boats moored along the beach. Borinquen Park consisted of a park and boulevard, the boulevard extending from where Indio Park sits today all the way to the outskirts of Ocean Park. I suppose that this boulevard was converted into a boardwalk further down by Punta Las Marías, which used to be known as Ciénaga de Machuchal and now is known as Barbosa Park or "Último Trolley." In a second postcard, on the left-hand side of the boardwalk, as it slopes to the beach, they have planted what appears to be a row of shrubs and areca palms. In the distance we see lampposts, which suggest that the park was used in the evening. To the left, they have constructed wooden buildings that block the ocean view. The buildings, with their angled roofs, are completely enclosed, making their purpose a mystery. The park visitors sit on benches with the same formality as in the previous postcard. No one is wearing a short sleeve shirt; they are all gentlemen. The second postcard also has the same proportion of more men than women, the females remaining in their "golden jails," according to the commentary of one of the principal North American chroniclers who arrived with the invasion. The place feels idyllic around Punta Las Marías; the forest of coconut palms has become dense and lush.

The possibility of a seafront, so often denied in our history of a city closed to the coastline, insinuates itself in these postcards, giving the city its marine metaphor. It was as if, for a moment, the imagined city met the real, then was erased, crossed out. Urban history, like personal history, is made from choices that are never carried out, choices that inspire a certain melancholic yearning, a desire for the life that could have been.

I think that today Ocean Park begins in the Kasalta Bakery, a gathering place that evokes the distant Kasalta of Havana, located at the extreme end of Miramar and serving as a marker and symbol of the rich neighborhood. When I went to the Kasalta in Havana, I recognized, in its ambition to convert itself into a sports bar in the style of a sad, socialist "Saturday night," its attempt to democratize the classes. In San Juan, Kasalta means something else altogether, as though its nostalgic imitation would have taken its job as a fast-food-style eatery to a new social level. What is interesting about Kasalta is the window display that makes the patrons look as if they are in a fish bowl. As they gather to talk trivialities, they seem to float because Kasalta is above all a gregarious place where we go to see and be seen, the paradise of the beach *flâneur* or the leisure-loving charlatan's chatting ground, the place where he can comment on women's behinds as well as condemn politicians, share eccentric schemes for how to make money, or boast about his bedroom exploits. The place stinks of middle age, though it is frequented by young women as well as old—in the latter case only after their first plastic surgery. They parade about, waiting to feel the butterflies that come from being desired, searching for them in a stranger's sideways glance or in the swagger of another's backside. Kasalta is where that particular type of despair exists that comes from always meeting the same people. Here the social gathering is more out of resignation than out of habit. It tries to be a European style café, but does not quite make it. We are seen, but we never feel the pleasure of watching the passersby because the sidewalks of Ocean Park are deserted and Calle McCleary hides a suburban calling. The *flâneur* lives here, facing the other patron at an oblique angle with respect to a city that requires the same urgency of attention as a mural or wall. For Manolo, my detective from *Sol de medianoche* and my facilitator in *Mujer con sombrero Panamá,* it is a place of clandestine meetings and confidences midway between his office and the street, the place of secret deals, the sanctuary for cultivating misanthropy or assisting in those crimes that arise from conscience wavering in the face of the law.

Calle Loíza contrasts greatly with McCleary. They run parallel yet remain foreign. While McCleary is a solitary street with few pedestrians on the sidewalks, Calle Loíza is Caribbean par excellence, evoking Calle de Diego in Río Piedras, a place of businesses, eateries, cheap restaurants, trinket shops, and Dominicans and Puerto Ricans on their way to finding bargains in Pitusa and Topeka. On Calle McCleary, the people seem to have found a refuge in Kasalta, while on Calle Loíza, the people seek the bustle of the street. Of all the eateries I visited in the eighties, I most remember Mutamba. Where is it? *Ubi Sunt?* It has gotten lost between the new Kentucky Fried Chicken and the Farrés Hardware Store. The owner of Mutamba was an Angolan, a former soldier, who appeared mysteriously on this street as an undocumented traveler. He was a tough man who marveled at the fact that beans with rice and minute steak with onions were as much from the Caribbean as from Africa. However, the Israel Liquor Store still remains the most recognizable place, the site Manolo—the real one, not the character—used to visit to quench his ravenous thirst and his anxieties with a morning beer. Tito was the philosopher of the place, with his little bottle of Volvic, which he always took to disguise his Vodka. In Mutamba one could imagine a conversation between Frank's brother Manolo, who was addicted to eateries, and Aurora, the Nuyorican with a nice ass, the vegetarian fiancée of Pat Boone, or was it Elvis Presley?

Ocean Park represents what is today a middle-class part of the city, though it used to be more aristocratic. It is joined to the working-class neighborhood of Villa Palmeras through a variety of streets that cross Calle Loíza from north to south. It is a route similar to Calle Calma, which is known today as Calle Ismael Rivera, where "El Sonero Mayor" (the great singer) was born, or to Calle Tapia, which counts the Hostería del Mar as its best place and crosses beneath Avenida Baldorioty de Castro and then climbs toward Villa Palmeras and Eduardo Conde, ending at the Casita Blanca Restaurant. They are gastronomic antipodes on the same street, the place where tabbouleh and falafel collide with goat fricassee or pig legs. These long streets are like old marriages, the adventure almost always occurs at the beginning; later comes boredom. At any rate, if we close our eyes and visualize old Cangrejos around the end of the nineteenth century, we note that on the north side, facing the beach, we turn our backs to the marshlands that climb toward the ridge marking the three hills of Santurce. The north-south axis of the streets represents the attempt to urbanize a contradictory landscape of paradoxical tastes. The view from the nearby coastline, favored by the developers of Borinquen Park, was preferable to the seduction of the panoramic view from the top of the hill. Where there was once swamp, mangrove, and marsh, it has now been filled, urbanized for the middle and upper classes. Where once there was a lookout point with a view of the ocean now stands Barrio Obrero and the working-class neighborhood of Villa Palmeras.

On Último Trolley Beach, so named not because it was the last streetcar stop but because it was where the last remaining wagon was utilized like a "rolling canteen," we once again recognize the possibility of a boardwalk. The Ocean Park suburb did not extend its sea wall there since it already ran to the Machuchal Marsh to the east. A place of heavy seas, strong erosion, and flooding, exactly where Barbosa Park stands today, Último Trolley remained clear and luminous for the contemplative view and the meditative walk. With time it would become the last evocation of what Borinquen Park was like in the early twentieth century. Punta Las Marías is further down, its pine forest marking the edge of the long arc of Isla Verde beach.

But before getting to Isla Verde, if we are traveling from the west, we see over our shoulder a surprising interruption or parenthesis in the cityscape—the low profile of the city stretching out to the sea, or, if we come from the east, we note instead the urban texture of the city itself. Like the San Antonio Bridge and the entrance to Condado, it is a place of clarity, of intense atmosphere, reminiscent of other cities and latitudes. In my opinion the Hostería del Mar, the same one in which Derek Walcott stayed when it was located in Condado, gives everything a North African flavor, probably just as much for its white color and low elevation as for its organic architecture achieved more through the successive layering of floors and rooftops than through any novel or uniform design. It resembles a temporary building on the shoreline, a living space that grew without excessively disturbing its setting. This lucent, horizontal quality of the city's last streetcar named desire remains threatened by the condominium that projects out toward the extreme west side of the beach, a beehive that would not only block the view of other lower condominiums but would also interrupt the arc of the marine landscape, which people have attempted to preserve with the recently restored marine boulevard. What vain desire of Puerto Rican urban planning that always privileges developers and privateers, seizing the

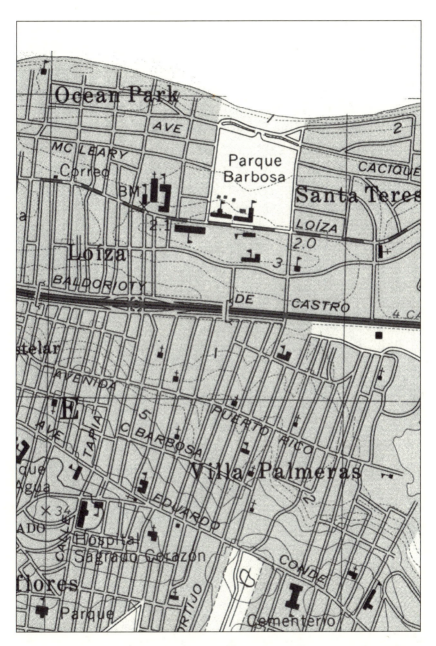

The north end of Calle Providencia (not labeled on this map) begins at Último Trolley in Ocean Park and runs south along the eastern edge of Parque Barbosa until it reaches the working-class neighborhood of Villa Palmeras.

little bit of common ground that is the shared urban landscape! I prefer to contemplate, to stretch out my view and imagine some tormented character of Camus walking the distant beach in Orán, another city looted by speculators and merchants.

We return to another of those streets that travel from north to south and enter into distinct areas. Calle Providencia begins at Último Trolley and continues along Barbosa Park, entering the Lloréns Torres housing project and passing by the neighborhood community center, then arriving at Avenida Baldorioty, crossing it, and finally climbing exhausted toward Avenida Eduardo Conde, the border between Villa Palmeras and Barrio Obrero. We start at the beach and climb toward the ridge of Cangrejos through Villa Palmeras, which was a semirural place covered in coconut palms at the beginning of the twentieth century. Only as the eastern end of the city became more developed did Villa Palmeras become more centrally located.

Calle Providencia connects Lloréns Torres, a public housing project from the fifties, with an older, working-class Santurce, a neighborhood that was developed at the beginning of the twentieth century. At another time, one could contemplate from that height an ominous sight even more remote in our history: the English fleet anchored in front of the San Juan coastline in 1797. The climb from the beach up Calle Providencia through the housing development to Eduardo Conde is a necessary one. It is like passing from mulattism to a memory of a blacker Puerto Rico, one that was more Afro-Caribbean, made up of runaway slaves and the lower class. It was exactly this reality of mulatto life and its ancestral memory that I tried to capture in *El entierro de Cortijo*. The funereal procession of the great *plena* musician was a journey toward the multiple histories of place. That is why in the middle of the book we enter into the scene between Chefa and the man with the ostentatious last name, Don Benicio Fernández Juliá. They were familiar anecdotes. Some of the men lived in the middle-class neighborhood of Monteflores and would go down to Villa Palmeras to take care of their lovers in the working-class neighborhood, "to burn petroleum," as they said in Havana. That old, Caribbean neighborhood, made out of historic and personal memory, drowned in its own brilliant northern light, is outlined in the map of that book saturated with the irony of a dispossessed *flâneur.*

Until two decades ago, one was able to glimpse here and there in Villa Palmeras the difficult passage from the slave barracks to the tenement houses. These two-story houses, with their long wooden or stone balconies and the rooms all in a row, contained part of a forgotten social history, where the abolition of slavery did not overcome the cruel overcrowding that today has been transformed into "public residential areas" or housing projects. Tenement homes, then, would be midway between slums and public housing. Like in the "Fourier Community" of Puerta de Tierra, the "Falansterio," they would test new ways of communal living for those in flight from abject poverty. The city contains the remains of an architecture that it wanted to transform time and again, the memory of a space occupied by bodies exhausted from work, forced into the oppressive despair of sharing a roof and being denied privacy.

By the "Playita" sector or neighborhood of Villa Palmeras, in front of the San José Lagoon, in my youth I frequented El Esquife Restaurant. They made a famous fried chicken, while the windows opened to the noxious odors of the lagoon. The dining room was enormous, recalling the metaphor of a wooden city made up of invisible tenement houses with long balconies sitting beside a lake, houses sprouting from mangrove trees and standing on stilts over the mud, a dreamlike place that I describe later in *Pandemonium,* a city somnolent in the scarce breeze, a place tormented by the sun's glare, the low-lying and dark mangrove swamp converting itself into the opposite of the limitless coastal landscape.

Avenida Baldorioty de Castro, which crosses at great speed the traditional world of Calle Providencia with its historic yet unseen tenement homes, the *casas de vecindad,* is explained in the most famous metaphor in Puerto Rican literature. I refer to the traffic jam

115

that appears in Luis Rafael Sánchez's *Macho Camacho's Beat*. It is also a world of erotic appetites that transcend social classes. Yet the promise of mobility, at least some sort of mobility, is never realized in that metaphor of the gridlocked society, the city that preferred the automobile to the pedestrian.

We turn back north, in the direction of the beach. We complete our walk along Último Trolley and arrive in Punta Las Marías, which is the neighborhood between Ocean Park and Isla Verde, a neighborhood also populated in the twenties and thirties by the beach-going desires of a bourgeoisie that had already begun working and benefiting under the North American regime. Some of these houses were owned by North Americans captivated by the tropics, like Dr. Charles H. Terry in Ocean Park, who swam the coastline and at times reached the cliff seen in the horizon from Último Trolley Beach. Other houses belonged to a Puerto Rican bourgeoisie with sumptuous appetites and provincial timidity. Somewhere between mansions and beach houses, these homes occasionally dreamed of Ionic or Doric columns decorating their entryways; it was the dream of a Belle Epoque in the middle of a coconut palm forest.

In the 1950s Pablo Casals arrived in this area between Punta Las Marías and Isla Verde. Already famous, and adored, Casals was taken about by the illustrious administration of Luis Muñoz Marín, only to become a symbol of a beach that back then was still a working-class spot with the dubious reputation that goes along with dance clubs by the sea. Don Pablo arrived with his pipe, his umbrella, his old age, the hope of his wife and pupil Martita Montañez, and, like a good Catalan, an enchantment with the sea. Time and again, he was photographed on that beach between Punta Las Marías and Isla Verde always defending himself with umbrellas from the scorching sun; he was an emblem of a musical, European culture that burst on the tropical scene of Benny Moré and Rafael Cortijo. The posters of the Casals Festival show the old man impeccably dressed in black, walking along the beach on his way to the concert hall. When not making publicity appearances, he would walk the beach, barefoot,

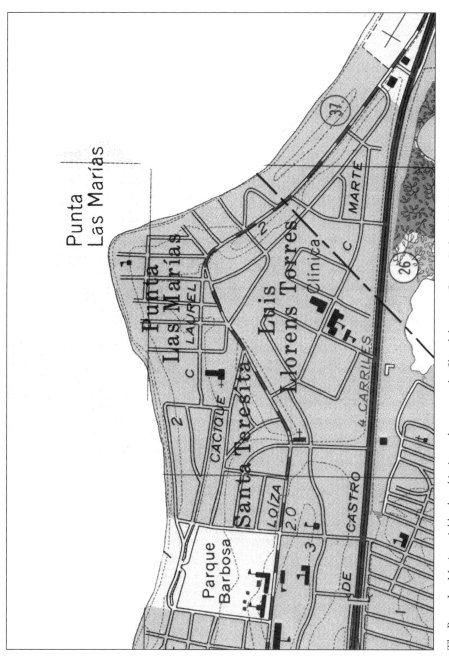

The Punta Las Marías neighborhood is situated on a stretch of beach between Ocean Park and Isla Verde.

yet still holding his umbrella, swift and stubborn, like so many quick-tempered Iberians. Cristóbal Ruiz painted him that way on the beach of Isla Verde, with his short-sleeved shirt, holding his umbrella like a wax candle, the blue of the nearly beatific ocean in the background. The painting served as a great symbol of that epoch, which included the foundation of the Casals Festival, the Symphony, the Music Conservatory, and San Juan's aspiration to be a city of culture in the European style.

In his memoir Casals confessed that he always wanted to live in a lighthouse beside the sea. He began to fulfill that desire long before moving to Isla Verde with the panoramic view of the sea from his house in San Salvador, Spain. But it was the enchantment of the sea of Isla Verde, a variant of *The Contemplated,* that so enraptured him, seducing him in his later years. That sea, he confessed, was bluer than the sea of San Salvador, its beauty and brilliance more captivating. In one photo, he appears in profile with his pipe, standing on what seems to be the terrace of his house in Punta Las Marías. The ornamental ironwork that was becoming popular on windows in the fifties and sixties appears rusty, eaten away by the salty air. The photo is taken against the light, allowing us to discover the radiance of the sea. In another photo he appears seated in a folding chair carrying his umbrella, his shoes off and pants rolled up, with Martita Montañez smiling at him.

11

The Arc of Isla Verde

There is something about Isla Verde that captivates me. It is probably its consistent vulgarity. Isla Verde has the distinction of a woman with rollers in her hair on Sunday night who knows that on Monday morning she will wake up just as ugly. It is a place blessed by the beauty of *The Contemplated,* but secretly it is seen as without cachet. Isla Verde suffers from low self-esteem. It is vulgar, not just because of its beach but because it is the "beach bum" of the city. People who sleep with the incessant beating of the waves suffer from boredom and are only cured by fleeting moments of pleasure. There is something sinister in the temporary and provisional nature of Isla Verde. It is the neighborhood that figuratively raised its huts on poles under the almond and coconut trees. Its anonymous architecture and its urban landscape of generic fast food and drive-thru eateries have the fugitive character of many of the inhabitants of the place. Isla Verde is like a short coconut palm that never gave shade. The palm tree could be made of brass and it would not make a difference; the beauty of the place is always an add-on, like that same woman who goes out on Saturday night with her hair in rollers, consoling herself with the fact that she has an ass like Jennifer Lopez. In reality, when Don Pablo Casals walked the arc of the long beach, it led him nowhere. It is exactly that: Isla Verde does not

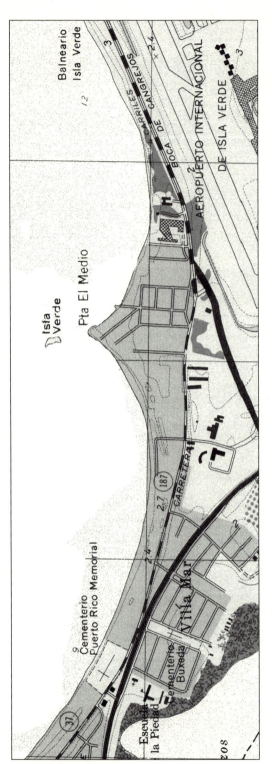

Isla Verde consists primarily of shoreline and lies north of the Luis Muñoz Marín International Airport. The beach of Isla Verde stretches from Punta Las Marías past Punta El Medio.

evoke anything that isn't itself. It is a unique place; it is "in your face," the middle-class ghetto anchored in the sand, without any other ambition than to plunder the marine landscape. Isla Verde can be cruel, even brutal. Perhaps it is only captivating for me because it reminds me of other beloved places. I must confess it: Isla Verde is an Avenida 65 de Infantería with a beach. My intimate and complicit love for her resides in the place where I came to cure myself of my turbid origin.

I complain of this, that, and the other thing—that the beach is besieged, the city ensnared, that they have privatized the view of the ocean. And I say nothing but bullshit because even still I love it; Isla Verde's ambition is authentic, original. It does not pretend to be Cadiz, like Old San Juan, Vedado like Miramar, or even Miami as Condado does. Like Iris Chacón, it could never appear on the cover of *Vogue*. We will leave that to Paris, to Juliette Binoche in any case. Isla Verde is the daughter of an Avenida Campo Rico who dreams of the people in *Hola* magazine. She yearns for a fairy-tale wedding, but without the nuisance of a man sleeping with her, screwing her every night. No one fucks with Isla Verde.

A fact that I am about to rectify. I do not want Isla Verde to have a marine boulevard after all! To hell with Havana's marine boulevard, or Santo Domingo's, or Copacabana's! What is most attractive is that when you are in the ocean swimming and you look back at that wall of condominiums, the whole, fucked island of Puerto Rico disappears. Isla Verde cultivates my contradictory misanthropy.

Isla Verde was never innocent for me. In the early fifties my neurasthenic mother was always complaining about this or that, but especially about the sand she found inside my father's Pontiac Catalina. The sand was from either Cecilia's or Mario's Restaurants, which used to be where the Marbella and Villas del Mar condominiums are today. Along with matchboxes from those establishments, the sand was decisive evidence that my father was fooling around with someone who, as she liked to say, was a "breezy lady." According to her menopausal imagination, loose women went to the bars at these restaurants and later, after walking awhile on the beach, slept with my father, in the process emptying their heels on the carpet of my father's Pontiac Catalina. It was a beautiful and paranoid image that endured in my imagination: the sand always revealed everything—less obvious than lipstick on the collar and more so than the other's scent on the genitals.

Isla Verde had a reputation as a place for "breezy ladies." I have a photo of Isla Verde from 1946, the year I was born to the rabid menopause of my mother, Acacia. The point of Boca de Cangrejos is in the distance. Closer in, we can see Punta El Medio, with its pine grove and coconut palm forest dotted with houses, where the run-down Empress Hotel sits today. Did one of the houses belong to the legendary Madamo? Further to the right, and almost flush with the ocean, we see some low-lying buildings, the beachside dancing halls of that era. Hidden among the pines is the famous Guadalquivir. It was there that Acacia surely invented the neologism "breezy lady." The place was also frequented by upper-class whites, who heard for the first time the sarcasm of these women of the world, their first bitches. From Punta El Medio, the little islet that is more properly called Isla Verde, there is a distance that has been made short through the years, the storms, and the heavy seas. The islet appears in the photo with a lone palm tree on the far right. It was there that Manolo supposedly buried the cruel weapon in *Sol de medianoche.* In the foreground we see the beach, what has now become the Marbella Condominium Complex. The sea is high, and at night we know there must have been a strong undertow because the entire beach is full of seaweed. It is possible that we are in the off season, the months whose names contain *r*'s, when the beach is desolate. The undertow reveals a solitary piece of deadwood, and if we are in the beginning of summer, the 20th of June 1987, forty-one years after this photo was taken, I am swimming from Boca de Cangrejos to Último Trolley in three hours and twenty-one minutes. Beyond the Fournier Cemetery, near Punta Las Marías, my swimming companion, Tony Puma, had an LSD flashback. He saw sharks all around us and took off. I swam like a son-of-a-bitch. You swam like the bastard you are, the other Manolo, the Pavía, told me later.

The postcards from the sixties still picture the coconut palms that extend from Punta Las Marías to the vicinity of what was known as Alambique Beach in the seventies because of its bayside pub; it was one of the notorious hangouts of that era. In a postcard taken from an aerial perspective—almost all of the postcards of Isla Verde are panoramas taken from a helicopter, from the point of view of the developer, the vultures—the horizontal and low-lying position of the old Hotel San Juan is emphasized by the bend in the arc of the beach where it almost touches Punta El Medio. The discrete architecture of the Hotel San Juan was a mirror of the Caribe Hilton, not so much in terms of its position as in its lines. The building stretches out elegantly in the manner of the tropical, hotel architecture used in the forties and fifties, calling to mind hotels such as the Jaragua Hotel in Santo Domingo and both the Tamanaco Hotel and the Humboldt Hotel in Caracas. The main building of the Hotel San Juan rose above the tops of the coconut palms, and then jutted out toward the islet of Isla Verde and Punta El Medio. The axis of the building ran north to south respecting the line of the beach. It was positioned so as to take advantage of the exuberant vegetation surrounding it and the beauty of the bay where the Guadalquivir used to be. In front of the old Hotel San Juan, on the beach just before the one called "la playita," there was a seaside bar that imitated the rural general stores of the forties and fifties. With red and white painted on its rustic doors, like the old Unión de Todos Restaurant in Barranquitas, and its corrugated tin roof, that bar resembled the dream of an alcoholic gringo stranded in the tropics. The tourism even pretended to be "typical" and picturesque, not international in the Howard Johnson style. The little bar lasted to the end of the seventies. Later they replaced it with a plywood absurdity ambitiously named "Victoria Station." And by the end of the eighties, with the restoration of the Hotel San Juan, the bar disappeared completely.

In a photo from the literary archive of Hunter S. Thompson, the author of *Fear and Loathing in Las Vegas* and *Rum Diary,* he appears to be lying on a lounge chair in the middle of Alambique Beach. In 1958, when Thompson lived in San Juan, Casals still took walks along the beach and might have run into that gringo par excellence snared by the tropics. And as soon as we arrive at that conclusion, doubt assails us regarding the place. The building in the distance appears to be the Hotel San Juan, yet it is too tall, and its enormity does not evoke the horizontality of the hotel, its soft setting. It could be one of the first condominiums . . . I don't know. The photograph leaves us perplexed. We almost think that it is the arc of the other beach, the public one, the *balneario.* In which case the hulking building in the distance would be beyond the Howard Johnson Hotel and the Pine Grove Condominiums. At the time of the late fifties, it was impossible that a building could exist in the curve of that other beach, even though Hunter S. Thompson—reclining across the chaise lounge in his bathing suit, sipping a drink, with his legs crossed and resting upon a rustic stool, a Corona beer symbolically placed to one side—seems to be on the shore below the terrace of the La Playa Hotel in Punta El Medio. The photograph is hard to place. It would seem to be an abbreviation or some type of symbolic collage made up of various places in the city, as happens so many times in *Rum Diary.*

Hunter S. Thompson lived in Puerto Rico in 1958, and in *Rum Diary* he was obsessed with the crowd of gringos—the bums as my annexionist father used to say—who started up *The San Juan Star* and who gathered together at Sam's Patio, La Botella, and El Batey. Some of the men acted like *pied noirs,* or better yet, like colonists in their scorn of a place they had come to because they were second-class citizens in their own countries. That resentment is made palpable in *Rum Diary* when Thompson speaks of San Juan. According to William Kennedy, the Pulitzer Prize–winning author of *Ironweed* and also a journalist for *The San Juan Star,* Hunter S. Thompson told him that he would do for San Juan what Hemingway's *The Sun*

Also Rises did for Paris, but in a "twisted way." The only difference between the two, apart from talent, would be that Hemingway loved Paris, and Hunter S. Thompson always detested San Juan.

In spite of his marked neurasthenia toward the city and frank antipathy toward Puerto Ricans, Thompson, who went on to become a celebrity of the so-called new journalism with books like *Fear and Loathing in Las Vegas,* did not have such a bad time on our beaches. The young reporter of the fictitious *San Juan Daily News* describes for us a sonorous fornication in what we think is Ocean Park Beach. In the last chapter of *Cartagena,* the character of Alejandro is about to do it on the beach of the Caribe Hilton, which seems like the same scandalous beach sex in this passage from Thompson's *Rum Diary:* "Rather than drive all the way out to the airport, where Sala said the beaches would be deserted, he turned off near the edge of Condado and we stopped on a beach in front of the residential section." He goes on, culminating in the seduction of Lorraine: "Suddenly she began to howl: at first I thought I was hurting her, then I realized she was having some sort of extreme orgasm. She had several of them, howling each time, before I felt the slow bursting of my own." After the howls in the sand, his neurosis returns and then the "mimis" become the source of his outrage with San Juan: "I was stung at least a thousand times by 'mimis'—tiny bugs with the jolt of a sweat bee. I was covered with horrible bumps when we finally dressed and limped back down the beach to where we had left Sala and his girl." The "mimis" are, of course, *mimes,* heroic insects in search of the pale skin of the conceited, ugly American. Spanish spelling is not Thompson's strong point in this book. He never understood, for example, that Caribe Hilton is written without an accent. In *Rum Diary,* it always appears as Caribé Hilton.

In *Rum Diary,* Hunter S. Thompson is more or less familiar with the San Juan coastline. In the strip from Old San Juan to the airport, he sketched out the map of his puckish adventures. He describes La Perla neighborhood with spite: "Often [Moberg] disappeared for days at a time. Then someone would have to track him down through the dirtiest bars in La Perla, a slum so foul that on maps of San Juan it appears as a blank space. La Perla was Moberg's headquarters; he felt at home there, he said, and in the rest of the city—except for a few horrible bars—he was a lost soul." Here, the stranded gringo recognizes the "dirty" gringo with a sarcasm like that of Bob McCoy. Hunter's scorn for San Juan is only surpassed by one of those Puerto Ricans stuck with an inferiority complex, someone like our former governor Carlos Romero Barceló in his famous interview in "Minority Minus One." As the legend goes, Barceló met Kate Donnelly around that time at Sam's Patio where the bitter gringos gathered to complain.

Nevertheless, Thompson has enough literary talent to sketch for us the important characteristics of San Juan at that time. In spite of describing meat-filled fritters as "pastillos" instead of "pastelillos" and the fact that "shots" of coco frío seem pure invention designed for an ignorant public, he reveals to us our enchantment with the automobile and sparkling, urban modernity, including the recent arrival of the television:

> I walked for more than a mile, thinking, smoking, sweating, peering over tall hedges and into low windows on the street, listening to the roar of the buses and the constant barking of stray dogs, seeing almost no one but the people who passed me in crowded autos, heading for God knows where—whole families jammed in cars, just driving around the city, honking, yelling, stopping now and then to buy pastillos and a shot of coco frío, then getting back in the car and moving on, forever looking, wondering, marveling at all the fine things the "yanquis" were doing to the city: Here was an office building going up, ten stories tall—here was a new highway, leading nowhere—and of course there were always the new hotels to look at, or you could watch the "yanqui" women on the beach—and at night, if you arrived early enough to get a good seat, there was a "televisión" in the public squares.

He now seems like a gringo who is frightened by these crazy Puerto Ricans.

At other times his characterization of the city would seem comic if it weren't for the disdain that animates it:

> Here I was, living in a luxury hotel, racing around a half-Latin city in a toy car that looked like a cockroach and sounded like a jet fighter, sneaking down alleys and humping on the beach, scavenging for food in shark infested waters, hounded by mobs yelling in a foreign tongue—and the whole thing was taking place in quaint old Spanish Puerto Rico, where everybody spent American dollars and drove American cars and sat around roulette wheels pretending they were in Casablanca. One part of the city looked like Tampa and the other part looked like a medieval asylum. Everybody I met acted as if they had just come back from a crucial screen test.

If Thompson would have stayed in San Juan for the rest of his life, he still would not have learned Spanish. He is a Malcolm Lowry without the tragic sense, rather with a certain Disneyworld foolishness.

Thompson needed an Eiffel Tower, or an Empire State Building, or the top floor of the Banco Popular for his view of San Juan. He needed a panorama of the entire coastline for his horseplay and perhaps he invented it: "Sanderson's office was on the top floor of the tallest building in the Old City. I sat in a leather lounge chair, and below me I could see the entire waterfront, the Caribé Hilton and most of Condado. There was a definite feeling of being in a control tower." Even though the gringo is not from the CIA, he still needs his "control tower," otherwise he is lost in the smallness of his own bitter ethnocentrism.

Isla Verde, Punta El Medio, the Hotel San Juan, and the Tropicoro Club roll around in the muddy residue of my psyche. The Tropicoro Club inside the Hotel San Juan appears in a postcard as a symbol of the tropical exoticism that dreamed of mulattas from the Tropicana Club in Havana. The sumptuousness of the nightclub, the elegance of the couples that seemed to witness the spectacle of the Spanish "Los Chavales" or "Los Churumbeles," is like an otherworldly call that summons the cabaret to inhabit our dreams. At this point I have to ask: What was the Hunca Munca? I suppose it was also a cabaret symbolic of the sixties, though I never went to it because of its exoticism and my allergy to easy hedonism. Somehow, because I never went there before it vanished, that cabaret will occupy a privileged place at my death. The Hunca Munca should be on my epitaph, the exotic place that I never visited out of fear of boredom. When I think about what lies beyond, I tell myself that I am going to the Hunca Munca, which is not the same as La Pianola, the cocktail lounge par excellence of the seventies known for its ballad music and romantic conquests. A guy named Oscar played the piano there, and I never thought that four years later in Punta El Medio, just steps away from La Playita because La Pianola was in the lower level of Hotel Playamar, I would drop anchor on my midlife crisis, barely thirty years old. I think about the Tropicoro, and I speak of the dream of the cabaret, I speak of the Hunca Munca, and I think of my death. . . .

Isla Verde is the beehive that hangs over the beach. An urban shoreline always signifies the frontier, a step in the opposite direction from the neurasthenia of the city, the hope for a cure that resides in the sea. The sea has its moods, but it is not restless; it is not anguished by time. One step from the boredom of its endless battle with the shore, the sea becomes an exercise in equanimity. The romantic soul sees in the ocean a symbol of its own tumultuous interior. Pursued by time, by the presentiment that my fearful nature had led me to make all the wrong choices, I went to the beach. There, Ivan Ilych's bed waited for me, winking. The beehive hovering over the beach, the incessant, hedonistic crowd became, for me, a crazy way to recover the conviction that I had lived.

The beach became a metaphor of my harsh and melancholic middle age. Swimming in the ocean, with each stroke, I reexamined, in that interior lens that only the swimmer understands, every imaginable desire. The ocean was also the space of erotic dreaming; desire is made more urgent by the sea's caress.

For that reason, in *Cartagena* you will go jumping over the hard, hot tar of Girona Street, in your bathing suit, on your way to crossing Alambique Beach, your heart drunk on Malcolm Lowry and a self-destructive impulse only healed by swimming. The "high" was in the way in which the sea twice caressed you, holding back all the manias of persecution at your disposal: sharks, barracudas, helicopters, and the people who ridicule you from the shore or who wait to give you back your damaged life—and your goal was the release of sex. The swim that marks the beginning of *Cartagena* finds its destiny in "Mexico, 1930," where thriving in the rapture of masturbation, in the phantasmagoria of the "flip card"—one woman in front and one from behind—was a way of living the illusion of that time. Because you smoked weed and still remained catatonic, beset by the beating of the waves and the crazy rejuvenation of that creamy three-in-the-afternoon light shining over the mountains of your childhood. The same way that alcohol awoke you to words and lucidity. The same way that the sedatives and all the other trash you exchanged for tobacco, for the Camel cigarettes, for the means of soothing the soap opera that you carry deep inside . . . The *Cámara secreta* was the sea and the Marbella Condominium the confessional for your sins. If *Cortejos fúnebres* was the map of your secret places, then *Cartagena* and *Cámara secreta* were your whispered confessions. You set up your tent there and watched as the wind lifted the awning, inflating it like our livers, while the *empanadas* cooked on the camping stove and Manolo stubbornly called deviled eggs "Egui-Joes." The Alambique was the beach of your Guggenheim Fellowship!

Head-trips are swims of their own. Your mind dissolves into spirit. Crossing that beach is like entering a foreign land; a strangeness dwells there that is part of the illusion of someone stranded in melancholy. The William Storryck of *Cortejos fúnebres* and *El cruce de la Bahía de Guánica* taught you to swim that beach, revealing to you its curative secrets. He smiled before that Puerto Rican dictum, the prohibition of the sea in the months containing the letter *r*. The best month to learn that beach, to attempt that undertow and those channels and cure yourself of fear, was November. William was a somewhat wayward Jew who learned to swim in Connecticut and loved the sea above all else. He attended to the office of alcoholism in El Batey and the bars in Vieques, but he also loved Isla Verde and its people. He was not allergic to Puerto Ricans. His neurasthenic gentleness and foreigner's solitude never metamorphosed into bitterness, and he always had the sea to soothe him.

Afterward you swam for a few years with Junior, a.k.a. Tony Puma, the veteran with a dishonorable discharge who never went to Vietnam and whose brain floated on acid, the visionary, the surrealist poet of sharks, and the man who said he would someday be the first Puerto Rican to scale Everest. To swim that beach with Tony was to jump into the absurdity of an insanity induced by acid and Rambo movies.

You swam with Kalman Barsy for many years, and, on the return trips, you walked the beach, sharing memories of the distant shores of South America. Kalman was a lifeguard in Argentina; his adolescent, beach adventures were turned into the novel *Verano*. Later you strolled upon the beach, and he recounted his novel *Naufragio* to you. You participated in the gestation of the book; it even served as a model for a scene of your own with Lady Catatonia as a character in silhouette. (Kalman appears as a Hussar who exchanged his sword for a Caribbean pirate's bandana. He complains that you resemble a third-rate lawyer with a bloated liver from drinking alcohol on the beach.) You knew, then, his most perfect novel, *La cabeza de mi padre,* even when it was nothing more than the seed we call anecdote. You swim with Kalman and you share his occupation with the sea and his literary ambition. Of course, there is the obvious incongruity of discussing literature half naked. The awkwardness of the albatross on land is part of the mark you share.

Then *Sol de medianoche* appeared, written in my friend Pedrín's apartment number five, behind the decrepit wooden gate and the garden wall, past the hollow where the soft drink machine was. They are small apartments painted hospital gray with white moldings. Back in the mid-eighties, in the apartment to the right, you found a gringo lost in the memories of Vietnam and drowning himself in alcohol, his Yankees cap the only tender detail from his life, and the vines, verdant and savage, climbing the walls, uniting the destiny of those lonely ones. With *Sol de medianoche* all the pieces of the puzzle fell into place: adultery, the beach, your parents, and your generation wavering between nostalgia and craziness. You told Kalman it was a mere exercise to see if you could write a "whodunit" novel. You wrote it, and everything was more mysterious than ever. The shoreline harbored the marginalized of the city, the narration a shelter for sad men who search for solace on the beach. Punta El Medio, like Villa Pugilato, is a risky compromise between divorce and rage, between separation from something or someone and the foolishness of Lady Prozac. In Punta El Medio's few streets, with their mocking names of flowers and faraway places, streets like Gardenia and Amapola, Iris, Dalia, and Girona alley, you walked among existentialist people with painful, at times comic, pasts.

Between the Condominium del Sol and Calle Amapola, there is a narrow alley that leads to a hidden beach where you can look out over the Pine Grove and public beaches. From there you see the terrace of La Playa Hotel, the rocky beach, the memory of the pier that was there in the seventies, the place where, perhaps, Hunter S. Thompson scribbled his notes. And beyond you have the islet of Isla Verde, where in 1946 there was a lone palm tree. When your muscles were weak, you used to go there in order to cross the arc of faith. You would swim at low tide, experience the first undertows, imprudent as you always were to start so early in the afternoon. You gave yourself baths, hydrotherapy for your frazzled nerves. You waited for twilight. The sun's glare, the rage, or the drunkenness were ways of escaping the little hospital, of leaving the cancerous gray with which Pedrín painted his houses. At that time, you had lost your head and were more worried about pleasure than art in a three-to-one ratio. You lived in drunkenness and lies that ensnared, a cesspool without end.

A mystery novel where the detective is a type of "beach bum" with a catholic education? That is how I conceived of *Sol de medianoche,* divining its tone, of course, from reading Chandler and writing restaurant reviews for the paper. The first paragraph of the review "El gusto de las tres Marías" gave me the crucial timbre for writing about indistinct streets and neighborhoods:

> The lower profile of the buildings on Avenida Américo Miranda and the infernal traffic remind me of my stubborn weakness for third-class neighborhoods. It is the type of avenue where the parallel streets are inevitably dedicated to garages and repair shops or to the criminal debuts of fifteen-year-olds high on crack. It is the type of "sexy" neighborhood where one goes to buy orthopedic shoes on a Saturday or to try on an inflatable prosthesis once the prostrate is shot.

The private detective's territory is the city, whether it is in the manner of Wilfredo Mattos Cintrón when he describes the public market of Río Piedras in *Desamores,* or Mayra Santos Febres when she shows us the neighborhood similar to Río Piedras as simply a place you pass by on your way to the run-down motel in *Cualquier miércoles soy tuya,* or when José Curet points out the *gámbaros* and labyrinthine passageways of the southern section of the old city. But I think that Isla Verde is the most suitable neighborhood for the private detective to plan his strategy for the search that will ultimately reveal the character of the city. Just as the sea surprises us because it is never the same, the city leaves us perplexed. Its many faces hide its heart, its character. In his novel *Como el aire de abril,* Arturo Echavarría uses Isla Verde as the compass of his investigation into the heart of the illicit, the immoral, into that which is sentimentally defective. And the beehives that line the beach from Punta Las Marías to the Hotel San Juan serve as a necessary background for the gaze that has as its object of curiosity the transitory nature of the bodies that move there in the windows of the opposite building, the victims of the spying camera or telescope. Here the nudity the voyeur searches for is only the beginning of that snooping into the mystery of urban secrecy:

How soon. He raised his gaze and scanned the floors of the nearest building. His apartment, in relation to the coast, was oriented at an angle, so that if he stood almost in front of it and a little to the right he would find the sea. If he looked to the left, his gaze would run into that massive pile of cement and glass that had been built some fifty meters from where he was staying in a high-rise where each apartment seemed to have a private balcony similar to his own. A variety of curtains over the windows denied access to the life inside while, in others, the lack of blinds on the doors and windows allowed one to occasionally observe figures in movement.

In *Historia de un dios pequeño,* Elidio La Torre Lagares picks Avenida Isla Verde as the place to begin his urban adventure. It is as if Isla Verde were free of virtues and full of *tapones,* or traffic jams, a place where the central metaphor of *Macho Camacho's Beat* reappears:

> There was an enormous traffic jam, and it was only nine at night. And it was all because someone driving down Avenida Isla Verde had an impulse to buy beer at the 7-Eleven and made an illegal left turn. The other driver, who was coming in the opposite direction, didn't feel like stopping and letting the first driver through. The impolite motorist's Mustang hit the first driver, as the first thought the other would wait for him. They remained copulating in the middle of the avenue, and neither moved his car until the police, who'd been stuck in the bottleneck, arrived. The "junkies" took advantage of the situation, selling antithetical roses and miniature Teddy Bears from window to window. Other drivers and their passengers simply got out of their cars to buy beer, rum, or vodka— whatever they could to baptize the night of the hypnotic moon of old blue cheese, and the radios blasted amplified and digitized memories that made the cars beat as if they had a heart. The anxiety, the calamity, and the swelling boredom drowned the common patience and everyone began to hit their horns, making the avenue sound like an out of tune orchestra.

I only object to the word "junkies." In Spain, they are called *yonquis* and in Puerto Rico, *tecatos.*

The third-rate detectives know more about cheap restaurants than fancy ones. They prefer pork chops to medallions. Georgie's in front of the Santa Teresita Church on Calle "Luisa," as Hunter S. Thompson would say, is the place for those who have fallen off the wagon. La Casita Blanca in Tapia is where the yuppies go when they want to be seen "slumming" it. Puerto Andín, in the tangle of mangroves that is Piñones, is a place the drug pushers would never take their women.

Apart from these gastronomic distractions, the neighborhood of Punta El Medio deserves further examination into the intimacy of its shade and the incitement to sleep in those streets where the sun's glare is cultivated only on the occasional corner, its harshness tempered by the branches of the acacias and the old flamboyán trees. Pedrín's houses on Girona, between Gardenia and Amapola, are refuges for sad men. Pedrín is a sort of priest-architect, attending to matters of the soul with his wise conversation and dealing with street matters with the urgency of a landlord. Without compromise, he builds housing that, according to Kalman Barsy, transforms his buildings into "living organisms." Pedrín is a master of making the most out of a small space. His supposition is that the tenant spends most of his time on the street, only eating, sleeping, and showering in the apartment—thus, needing a small space. Only those who are divorced or victims of adultery—their conscience diminished by obsession—can live in such reduced spaces. As a result, Pedrín's favorite tenants are the pilots from the nearby airport. When occupied by sexual athletes, the houses are shocked. The high walls that lend a false sense of privacy are not enough to temper the screams, moans, and squeaking mattresses. Now, as in any monastery, more than lust, despair and sadness saturate the air in this tenement house turned infirmary for souls. But it is the famished wolf of desire that howls the most.

In order to escape the screams, the torment of listening to another's desire without being able to taste it themselves, Manolo and Alejandro swam to the islet. And there they entered into a sort of catholic fervor. They would pray three "Our Fathers" and three "Ave Marias," bury the weapon or the body of their offense in the sand in order to alleviate their conscience, considering the sin and forgetting the crime, commending themselves to the Virgen of those who have no one. To look from the islet of Isla Verde—the same one that in 1946 only had one palm tree—is to leave the beehive, and, distancing yourself from it, to taste the islet of solitude facing the cursed Isla Verde, to alienate yourself from all of that, in any case, to rescue your soul, to look inward toward all that is good. To swim to the islet is to resist society.

Roland Barthes returns to remind me: In Punta El Medio there were two houses that appealed to me as good places to live the moment I saw them. They evoked in me phantasmal desires of previous lives, uncontrollable passions that stirred my insides. One was the ramshackle "green house" of the Iranian who was champion of Greco-Roman wrestling and who was stranded in the sleepiness of Punta El Medio by some mysterious deed forgotten in the fog of his insanity. The Cape Sea Village Condominiums remain there today. But back then the house was abandoned, invaded by a physically formidable squatter wearing red sweatpants. The house was painted green with white trim and molding. It had a balcony and a terrace that opened to a neglected and shaded garden with a garage and a platform with a wooden railing that looked over the palms, Maltese crosses, and canary shrubs below. The four-sided tin roof dated back to the thirties and forties. From the house I caught a glimpse of one of the beachside mansions that still stood at the edge of development many years after Muñoz Marín lived in this Isla Verde neighborhood. In *Cortejos fúnebres* I describe the green house of the Iranian Hashemi:

> On the corner of Rosa and Gardenia, the long balcony of the green house opens to the morning light. Alejandro remembered the first time he visited. It was a Sunday, around ten in the morning. The tepid morning sun had scarcely shone upon the canary creepers; the yellow flower hadn't yet wilted. It was only much later that the

135

sun's rays finally fell upon the shaded corner of the garden where Dr. Hashemi Bani Sadr greeted the new day with exercises, meditations, and prayers. Someone had recommended him to that Iranian shaman stranded in the slumbering tropics of Isla Verde.

The other house is on Calle Dalia and is a copy in miniature of Thomas Jefferson's Monticello. If the green house was the place where you would have desired to live the bohemian life during the forties, having been born in 1910, then the other house, the one that supposedly belonged to the political historian Bolívar Pagán, is like a Voltairian, rationalist fantasy set in the middle of the dense, Caribbean foliage. Its beauty lies in reconciling the exuberant, tropical vegetation with neoclassical lines that dream only of themselves. From its hidden location within the urban texture of San Juan, no one could approach its nostalgic architectural desires. It is exactly that secret solitude that turns the house into the ideal place for the renowned writer, en route to being read by children and adolescents.

12

The City and the Forest

Beyond Luis Muñoz Marín International Airport and the long stretch of beach that highlights the shoreline, beyond Boca de Cangrejos Bridge, from which one can see the entire coast of San Juan, you can find Piñones, a place of mangroves and the secret lagoons of Piñones and Torrecillas, which are truly the aquatic forests of the city, its forgotten destiny. At the city's edge, Piñones is thriving with coconut palms and pines planted long ago to break the hurricane-force winds; it is indeed an almost savage place.

Piñones is also the site of Puerto Andín: "Behind the barracks and to the right, and when you are about to fall in the canal, there it is . . ." The city cultivates places like these, places somewhere between the clandestine and the criminal, with restaurants, stalls, kiosks, bars, dives, and brothels, the trail you leave behind the same as the loneliness that pursues you.

You do not want to go to Vacía Talega or Piñones Lagoon, with its gray, muddy water and low swells almost flush with the well-kept grass and its ancestral population of blacks descended from runaway slaves. Today you will stay close to the city; you won't risk the adventure of the boy who, by living in Piñones could be living in Africa, because San Juan, as seen from Piñones, looks like a shimmering beacon of white by the sea, a magnificent splendor reaching to the sky.

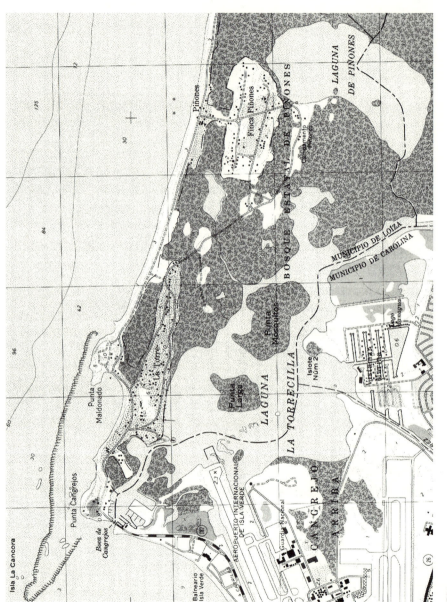

Piñones.

You stay there and remember the passage from your novel *Mujer con sombrero Panamá:* "It's like the old bastard told me: 'Puerto Andín is the place you bring a girl when you want to impress her; it's a place, you notice, that is real nature, and she starts thinking, shit, this guy knows about these things.'"

Later you insist that it is a secret place:

It's a private space, a place for drinking with a friend, for sharing painful secrets. One of the smaller shacks, with a corrugated tin roof and aluminum walls, was furnished with old pieces from the living room of a house on Avenida Puerto Rico. The furniture is covered with plastic, barely fulfilling its function under the incandescent sun of the canal, abandoned to the scarce breeze and the miasma of the mangrove. I'm only aware of these things. I don't hear the people near me.

Later you sit in Manolo's preferred seat to overcome the stupor of *jibarita* (marijuana), what we today call "cripy":

That barber's chair is also there in this shack, and I ask myself if I should sit awhile in order to pacify my nerves—be cool, *gardez votre calme, coge por la sombrita.* Unexpectedly I'm confronted with my own deficiency. The feeling assaults me with an urgency, perturbing me. Nowhere do I feel more like a child than in the barber's chair. I sit. The paralysis overcomes me.

Manolo could appear in the next novel, smoking cripy from the fierce adolescent under his tutelage and remaining in the barber chair, stupefied, convinced that the fish broth in his stomach is Lake Titicaca, just like what happened to you at the Flamingo on the 65 de Infantería over the bar stools after having devoured a huge shrimp stew.

Or you could then go to one of the better places in Piñones, the bar known as The Reef, and not eat the *alcapurrias* to cure yourself of the munchies. And you would think that in reality there are two Mulholland Drives in San Juan. David Hockney may not have described them, but they both offer aerial views, one from the promontory, the other from the mountain. And the city below remains a passive protagonist, at last delivered from the daily grind and converted into a character.

You arrived at The Reef during the night. Billiard balls crack with the insistence of this place, the place you would visit before a suicide. If Hunter S. Thompson would have known The Reef, he might have remained there, a bartender telling tales, until he came to love Puerto Rico and Puerto Ricans. From the promontory where The Reef sits, you look out over the splendor of the city, the darkness of the ocean that harbors it, the long coastline plagued by illuminated buildings, appearing like a cruise ship that does not dare weigh anchor because it is obsessed with persecution.

The Lomita Sector in Los Filtros, Guaynabo City, is yet another place you can only get to by car, though the climb is a tortuous one. But there, as you know, instead of the desperate, you will find the rich. When they take their Rottweilers and German Shepherds out for a walk at dusk, the city lies below, the space of their dominance, of their ambition. During the day they watch the city, and she seems to work for them. At night they contemplate the city, and it seems that they illuminate her. La Lomita is the place where pleasant philanthropy lives and crack cocaine never makes it past the private security guards.

The Reef is the complete opposite: From there, you gaze out at the city below, and you cannot admit that those beehives of people where the city surrenders itself to the daily flurry of eating and defecating, washing and procreation, love and hate are truly Sodom. With three gins in your head, you think about adolescence as the incessant search for pleasure, middle age as a coup d'état, and old age as a crazy desire for the future, for immortality. You tell yourself that down there is sin, the world, and here, above, the despair of philosophy. You repeat it to yourself. From above, from the promontory of the prophet, all cities are Sodom and Gomorrah. A panorama carries the curse of metamorphosing the city into an object of your judgment. And he who judges worst fails best. That is also true, and you are the first to admit it. Let them remain below, eating and shitting, snorting coke and smoking crack, fucking furiously and popping out babies, pissing Lasix before the dope test, cracking bricks and lighting cigs, dying, shooting, being born, reading Coelho, teaching Foucault, singing salsa, praying, thinking, studying, doing aerobics and visiting the Plaza Las Américas, above all creating trash, sampling sushi, and praising Tego, swimming in fifty meters of pure shit. You should abandon The Reef. Since you do not have the equanimity of philanthropy, the vision of San Juan from those heights transforms you into a misanthrope. Soon enough you will join Hunter S. Thompson in his contempt for the "medieval asylum" restored by the song "Alegría bomba é." Get down from that dangerous mountain.

13

The Bridge

Manolo will always return to Río Piedras and Calle de Diego, following the route from *Mujer con sombrero Panamá*, taking the Moscoso Bridge over the San José Lagoon, turning his back on Isla Verde and Piñones. In the afternoon, when the water is no longer calm, when it no longer reflects the titanium light so abundant in the morning, Manolo curses the rippling flags of the Commonwealth of Puerto Rico that fly over the Moscoso Bridge, the metaphor of the bridge between two cultures, between the colony and the metropolis, between the mistake and the misunderstanding. And he also cries out against the so-called sands of the Sahara, or the tsunamis forecast for Último Trolley Beach. "Tell me when in the hell did we speak in this country of the sands of the Sahara or the fucking tsunami?" San Juan acquires exotic habits. They have sushi bars there, the sands of the Sahara and the tsunami being the principal recipients of Manolo's fury.

Anyway, Manolo revs the accelerator on his Malibu 71 as he rips through the pavement of the fucking Moscoso Bridge, his Hawaiian shirt snapping in the wind, his long-haired dachshund sticking its head out the window, taking in the panorama, and Commander Carabine sitting in the back of the convertible, slumped over, asleep, his liver filled with 70 percent THC. And everything is shrouded in the ocean's haze, or in the sands of the Sahara. It is what your mother called the sun's glare. The distant hills are erased, and the Falú subdivision to the left is a monument to oblivion. Everything from here to El Yunque is blurred in the smoky haze.

Manolo knows all that, and he knows that this city of buildings that seem to sprout from the mangrove swamp is so young that it has forgotten its recent past with its view to the sea or the pestilent canal. It was a city suddenly inhabited by the mountain *jíbaros,* who, dreaming of cities further to the north, beyond the seas, embarked on the Marine Tiger or Pan American Clippers. They were uprooted peasants, who had no desire for a city by the sea. The poverty of the canal and the lagoons was theirs alone. The view to the sea was a privilege ceded to the rich. The city remains in a provisional state, without its metaphors, without narcissism. Yet San Juan has a spontaneous, natural beauty typical of a woman who appears gorgeous at six in the morning, desirable even with rollers in her hair, a half-made-up woman who invites a tender gaze.

If there is no metaphor, there is no narcissism, and if there is no narcissism, there is no mirror because every beautiful city has a metaphor in which it sees itself—that of the river or beach, the hill or lake, the mirage of the desert or the reflection from the waters of the lagoon. The city's delight in itself is cultivated through that metaphor; there resides its contemplation.

San Juan needs a vision. The stilt shacks in Nueva Venecia rise toward the sky, aerial housing projects growing upward from the lagoons, and, in the distance, a Simon Rodia–style tower of melancholic lucubration. More than the urban metro, the city needs the vision of Niño Avilés for the mangroves, period.

The history of this city has been primarily rural, territorial, and utilitarian, its resources abandoned like roots in the field. San Juan never succeeded in claiming its raison d'être. It is for that reason that Manolo returns to the ordinariness of Calle de Diego and Avenida 65 de Infantería. In those places the pain of loss is raw. It does not need the philanthropy of do-gooders or the misanthropy of rancorous writers. Only there does San Juan preserve its cutting edge, only there can the city be itself.

Glossary of Names

COMPILED BY PETER GRANDBOIS

Alberti, Rafael (1902–99): A Spanish-born poet and painter identified with the avant-garde, particularly abstract painting, cubism, and surrealism. At the end of the Spanish Civil War, he fled to Argentina only to return to his homeland after Franco's death.

Alberty, Roberto "El Boquio" (1930–85): One of the key figures in the history of contemporary Puerto Rican art, noted for his surrealist and Dadaist tendencies. His artistic production was intimately related to his literary work, primarily as a poet.

Albizu Campos, Pedro (1891–1965): President of the Nationalist Party in Puerto Rico. He staunchly opposed the assimilation and annexation of Puerto Rico to the United States.

Althusser, Louis (1918–90): A French Marxist who saw Marxism as a science. He suffered from periodic bouts of mental illness, which may have contributed to the fact that he strangled his wife, the revolutionary Hélène Rytman, to death in 1980.

Balseiro, Puchi (1925–2007): A Puerto Rican singer/songwriter and radio/TV producer born into a musical family as Áurea Mercedes Balseiro but best known as "Puchi" Balseiro.

Barsy, Kalman (1942–): A Hungarian-born writer who has lived in Puerto Rico since 1974. He is a professor of language and literature at the University of Puerto Rico.

145

Barthes, Roland (1915–80): A French literary critic, social theorist, philosopher and semiotician. His works include *Mythologies* and *S/Z*.

Baudelaire, Charles (1821–67): One of the most important French poets of the nineteenth century. His most famous volume of poems is the controversial *Les Fleurs du mal,* for which the author and his publisher were prosecuted for its scandalous themes of death and sex.

Belaval, Emilio S. (1903–73): A distinguished Puerto Rican who graduated from law school in 1927 and went on to become a writer, essayist, dramatist, lawyer, and journalist.

Benítez, Lucecita (1948(?)–): A singer who was part of the new wave of Puerto Rican popular music. Born Luz Esther Benítez, but better known to the world as Lucecita Benítez, her first major hit was "Un lugar para los dos."

Betances, Ramón Emeterio (1827–98): The primary leader of the Grito de Lares revolution (the first major attempt to overthrow the Spanish in Puerto Rico). He received a Doctor of Medicine degree from the University of Paris but returned to Puerto Rico to establish a hospital only to become deeply involved in the revolution.

Binoche, Juliette (1964–): A French movie actress famous for such films as *Chocolat* and *The English Patient.*

Blanco, Tomás (1897–1975): A San Juan–born novelist and literary critic. He also studied medicine at Georgetown University.

Boquio, El. *See* Alberty, Roberto "El Boquio"

Bousoño, Carlos (1923–): A Spanish poet and critic who has published many volumes of criticism and poetry.

Brown, Willard (1915–96): An outfielder in the Negro Leagues and Major League Baseball; nicknamed "Home Run."

Burgos, Julia de (1917–53): The best-known female poet in Puerto Rico. Rodríguez Juliá is suggesting that Ángela María Dávila's poetry was influenced by Julia de Burgos.

Cabán Vale, Antonio (1942–): A poet, composer, and singer, best known for his Puerto Rican folk songs; nicknamed "El Topo."

Campeche, José (1752–1809): The first major Puerto Rican artist of note. He is considered the founder of Puerto Rican national painting.

Camus, Albert (1913–60): An Algerian-born French writer and philosopher who won the Nobel Prize for literature in 1957. His most famous work is *The Stranger.*

Capó, Bobby (1922–89): A noted Puerto Rican singer, composer, and TV director, born as Félix Manuel Rodríguez Capó.

Carmoega, Rafael (1894–1968): One of the most famous architects in Puerto Rican history. Carmoega graduated from Cornell University in 1918. In addition to the Puerto Rican capitol, he designed many other buildings including the School of Tropical Medicine and the University of Puerto Rico.

Casals, Pablo (1876–1973): A Catalan cellist and conductor. In 1956 he settled in San Juan, where he lived out the remainder of his years.

Chacón, Iris (1950–): A Puerto Rican singer and vedette.

Chandler, Raymond (1888–1959): An American writer born in Chicago but raised in England. He became a renowned crime fiction writer and is especially famous for his descriptions of Los Angeles in the Philip Marlowe novels.

Clemente, Roberto (1934–72): A Major League right fielder elected to the Hall of Fame posthumously in 1973.

Clifford, Charles (1819–63): A Welsh-born photographer of Spanish scenery and architecture.

Cobb, Jimmy (1929–): A legendary American jazz drummer who played with such greats as Miles Davis and John Coltrane.

Coelho, Paulo (1947–): A Brazilian-born writer most famous for works such as *The Alchemist* and *Zahir*.

Coll, Yvonne (1947–): A model and film and television actress born in Fajardo, Puerto Rico.

Corretjer, Juan Antonio (1908–85): One of the greatest poets of twentieth-century Puerto Rico. He befriended Pedro Albizu Campos and became Secretary General of the Nationalist Party. He was jailed for his political ideas on many occasions.

Corso, Gregory (1930–2001): An American beat poet who was part of the group that included Jack Kerouac and Allen Ginsberg.

Cortijo, Rafael (1928–82): A Puerto Rican musician, bandleader, and composer, born and raised in the neighborhood of Santurce. He quickly became one of the most important Plena music stars, his name synonymous with Puerto Rican identity. Rodríguez Juliá writes about him in his chronicle *Cortijo's Wake*.

Crowe, George (1921–): A first and second baseman out of Indiana who played for nine years in the National League.

Cuba, Joe (1931–): A New York–born Puerto Rican musician considered by many to be the father of Latin "Boogaloo." Born as Gilberto Calderon, his most famous song is generally considered to be "El Pito," or "I'll Never Go Back to Georgia."

Curet, José (1949–): The author of *Crimen en la calle Tetuán,* in which he describes the *gámbaros* and labyrinthine passageways of the old city of San Juan.

Curet Alonso, Catalino "Tite" (1926–2003): An internationally respected songwriter raised in the Barrio Obrero section of Santurce.

Davis, Miles (1926–91): One of the most influential and innovative jazz musicians—best known as an accomplished trumpet player—in the United States in the twentieth century. His album *Bitches Brew* is famous for its fusion of rock and jazz.

Delano, Jack (1914–97): A Russian-born American photographer who traveled to Puerto Rico in 1941 to chronicle the poverty there as part of the Farm Security Administration. The trip had such a profound effect on him that he settled in Puerto Rico shortly thereafter.

del Villard, Sylvia (1928–90): An actress, ballerina, choreographer, and Afro–Puerto Rican activist born in Santurce.

Díaz, José "Pepe" (?–1797): A sergeant major who led the Toa Alta militia against the English and was killed near the Martin Peña canal in 1797.

Díaz Valcárcel, Emilio (1929–): A Puerto Rican writer born in Trujillo Alto. His most recent work is a collection of stories titled *Cuentos completos.*

di Benedetto, Antonio (1922–86): An Argentinean journalist and writer most famous for his existentialist masterpiece *Zama,* published in 1956.

Diego Padró, José I. de (1899–1974): A poet who, together with Luis Palés Matos, created the literary avant-garde movement known as "Diepalismo."

Dipiní, Carmen Delia (1927–98): A Puerto-Rican singer who is most famous for her boleros.

Diplo (1909–56): A Puerto Rican idol born as Ramón Rivero. With his popular comedy and through his famous character "Diplo" he entertained Puerto Rico for more than thirty years.

Ellroy, James (1948–): A Los Angeles–born crime fiction writer perhaps best known for the film *L.A. Confidential,* which was based on his book of the same name. *The Black Dahlia,* another Ellroy novel about L.A. crime, was made into a film in 2006.

"Enjuto," or Federico Enjuto Ferrán (1884–1965): A judge and father of four children, one of whom is Jorge Enjuto. In 1936, in the midst of the Spanish Civil War, Judge Federico Enjuto Ferrán condemned José Antonio Primo de Rivera to death.

Enjuto, Jorge. *See* "Enjuto"

Enríquez [Henríquez], Miguel (1680–?): A Puerto Rican shoemaker turned pirate who fought the British in Vieques.

Fanon, Frantz (1925–61): A French psychiatrist and revolutionary writer born in Martinique and a descendent of African slaves. Fanon rejected his teacher Aimé Césaire's concept of "Négritude," asserting instead that a person's identity depended on their economic and social status.

Feliciano, José "Cheo" (1935–): A Puerto Rican–born singer. At seventeen he moved with his family to New York where he began his career as a percussionist, later singing in bands with Tito Rodríguez and Joe Cuba.

Fellini, Federico (1920–93): An Italian filmmaker who is widely considered one of the most influential directors of the twentieth century. He was famous for mixing dreams, memories, and fantasies into his narratives, which are often personal if not autobiographical. His films include *La Strada, La Dolce Vita, 8½,* and *Satyricon.*

Ferré, Luis A. (1904–2003): An engineer, industrialist, politician, and philanthropist, and governor of Puerto Rico from 1969 to 1973. He was also the founding father of the New Progressive Party, which advocated statehood.

Ferré, Rosario (1938–): Puerto Rico's leading woman of letters. Born in Ponce, she has taught at Harvard, Berkeley, Rutgers, and Johns Hopkins University among others. Her most famous book is *The House on the Lagoon.*

Figueroa, Guillermo (?–2001): Part of a famous musical family. The three brothers, Guillermo, Kachiro, and Rafael, were all part of what many consider the first family of Puerto Rican music. They played together in what was known as the Figueroa Brothers Quintet.

Figueroa, Jaime "Kachiro" (1912–2003). *See* Figueroa, Guillermo

Figueroa, Rafael (1914–). *See* Figueroa, Guillermo

Flax Hjalmar (1942–): A poet, educated as a lawyer, who has published eight volumes of poetry.

Foucault, Michel (1926–84): A French philosopher noted for his influence in the realms of psychiatry, medicine, and literature. He was most often associated with the structuralists.

Fourier, Charles (1772–1837): A French utopian, socialist thinker who advocated communal living, among other things.

García Márquez, Gabriel (1928–): The Nobel Prize–winning author of *One Hundred Years of Solitude, Chronicle of a Death Foretold, Love in the Time of Cholera,* and many others. He is, perhaps, the most famous of all Latin American writers.

García Ramis, Magali (1946–): A Puerto Rican novelist and professor at the University of Puerto Rico.

Garnier, Tony (1869–1948): Considered one of the forerunners of twentieth-century architecture.

Gibson, Joshua (1911–47): Born in Georgia and considered the greatest power hitter in black baseball. He died just three months before baseball became integrated.

Ginsberg, Allen (1926–97): An American beat poet of the same generation as Corso and Kerouac. He is best known for his poem *Howl.*

González, José Luis (1926–96): One of the most famous and most important of Puerto Rican writers. He was born in the Dominican Republic to a Dominican mother and a Puerto Rican father. He later became a citizen of Mexico. His novels, short stories, and essays have been widely translated and anthologized.

Granell, Eugenio Fernández (1912–2001): One of the most important Spanish cultural figures of the twentieth century. He was a musician, writer, sculptor, and, above all, a painter. He was considered a surrealist like his friend and teacher André Breton.

Guevara, Ché (1928–67): An Argentinean-born Marxist revolutionary. Ernesto "Ché" Guevara originally studied medicine but went on to support Castro in his bid for power in Cuba. Guevara was captured and executed by members of the Bolivian Army.

Guillén, Jorge (1893–1984): A Spanish poet, member of the Generation of '27, and friend of Pedro Salinas. He was in exile in the United States from 1932 to 1938.

Guillén, Nicolás (1902–87): An Afro-Cuban poet, writer, journalist, and social activist.

Gutiérrez Vega, Hugo (1934–): A Guadalajara-born poet who has worked as the Mexican ambassador to Greece and the rector of the Universidad Autónoma de Querétaro.

Hernández Acevedo, Manuel (1921–88): Considered to be one of the grand masters of "naive art" in Puerto Rico. Born in Auguas Buenas, where he only completed the fourth grade, Hernández Acevedo was later inspired by other artists to portray popular scenes, events, and places in his works.

Hockney, David (1937–): A British painter, draughtsman, printmaker, and photographer.

Howard, Frank (1936–): A former outfielder, first baseman, coach, and manager in Major League Baseball.

Iglesias, César Andreu (1915–76): A writer who was one of the founders of the Puerto Rican Independentista Party in 1946 and persecuted as a Communist during the McCarthy era.

Isherwood, Christopher (1906–86): An Anglo-American novelist, poet, and playwright known for his novels about Berlin in the early 1930s, including *Goodbye Berlin*.

Jiménez, Juan Ramón (1881–1958): A Spanish poet born in Moguer in Andalusia. One of his most important contributions to poetry was the idea of "pure poetry." He opposed Franco in the Spanish Civil War and fled to Puerto Rico in 1939.

Juliá, Raul (1940–94): An actor born in Puerto Rico who went on to become a Hollywood star. He is known particularly for such films as *Kiss of the Spider Woman, Romero,* and *The Addams Family.*

Kalman. *See* Barsy, Kalman

Kaye, Danny (1913–87): An American actor, singer, and comedian. He is perhaps best known for his role in the film *The Secret Life of Walter Mitty.*

Kennedy, William (1928–): An American writer and journalist and the Pulitzer Prize–winning author of *Ironweed.*

Kerouac, Jack (1922–1969): Perhaps the best-known writer of the American Beat scene. His most famous works are *On the Road* and *The Dharma Bums.*

Klumb, Henry (1905–84): A German architect who arrived in Puerto Rico via the United States after studying with Frank Lloyd Wright. He was largely responsible for leading the transition in San Juan from Spanish Revival to a more modern vision. Most of his buildings were designed between 1945 and 1965.

Krupa, Gene (1909–73): A famous and influential jazz drummer. At one point he played with Red Nichols's band.

Kurosawa, Akira (1910–98): A prominent, award-winning Japanese film director and producer. He is widely considered one of the masters of the cinema. His most famous films include *The Seven Samurai* and *Ran.*

La Torre Lagares, Elidio (1963–): A poet, essayist, and novelist born in Adjuntas, Puerto Rico.

Laguerre, Enrique (1905–2005): A well-known Puerto Rican writer, poet, teacher, and critic. He has often been considered for the Nobel Prize in literature.

Levitt and Sons (c. 1965): The first developers in the history of Puerto Rico. They built tens of thousands of modestly priced homes. They were also the first developer to offer financing, sometimes with no down payment. Their style of business was modeled on that of the United States and, thus, was one of the first examples of the "progress" Rodríguez Juliá later mentions.

Lloréns Torres, Luis (1876–1944): A Puerto Rican poet, journalist, playwright, and politician who studied law in Spain and is most famous as a poet. His poems are nationalistic and known as *criollismo* because they take the customs and traditions of the island as their theme.

Lopez, Jennifer (1969–): A New York–born singer and actress of Puerto Rican descent.

Lowry, Malcolm (1909–57): A British writer who spent much time traveling through Mexico. *Under the Volcano* is his most famous novel.

"Madamo," or Madamo Díaz: A man in the Punta El Medio neighborhood with some notoriety.

Magritte, René (1898–1967): A Belgian-born artist who often made use of bowler hats in his surrealist paintings, such as *The Son of Man.*

Marques, René (1919–79): A renowned short story writer and playwright born in Arecibo, Puerto Rico. *The Oxcart* is widely considered his best play.

Martinez Nadal, Rafael (1877–1941): A journalist, lawyer, and politician, ultimately known as a pro-statehood senator.

Mays, Willie (1931–): An American icon widely regarded as one of the finest players ever to have played baseball. He was elected to the Hall of Fame in 1979.

Mineo, Sal (1939–76): An American actor and theater director most famous for his Academy Award–nominated performance opposite James Dean in *Rebel Without a Cause.*

Monroig, Glenn (1957–): A Puerto Rican composer and singer who burst onto the music scene in the early 1980s.

Montañez Martinez, Martita (1937–): Second wife of Pablo Casals.

Moré, Benny (1919–63): A Cuban musician famous for his boleros.

Muñoz Marín, Luis (1898–1980): Puerto Rico's first elected governor (1949). Educated at Georgetown University and having spent most of his youth in the United States, he returned to Puerto Rico determined to improve the plight of the country's poor. His nickname was "el Vate" (the bard) because he was also a poet.

Naipaul, V. S. (1932–): A Trinidad-born, 2001 Nobel Prize winner in literature. His books include *A House for Mr. Biswas* and *A Bend in the River.*

Nechodoma, Antonin (1877–1928): An architect who was born in Prague but eventually settled in Puerto Rico.

Neruda, Pablo (1904–73): A Chilean writer and communist politician. The real name of this world-renowned and Nobel Prize–winning poet is Ricardo Eliecer Neftalí Reyes Basoalto. Neruda has become the most widely read of Latin American poets.

Newman, Francisco "Papo": A hired killer who participated in the assassination of the Puerto Rican television host Luis Vigoreaux on January 17, 1983. He confessed to the crime and later expressed regret, blaming his actions on his drug addiction.

Nichols, Red (1905–65): An American jazz musician. He was the son of a music teacher and by the age of 12 was playing cornet with his father's brass band. He became one of the leading jazz musicians of the age, headlining with his band "Red Nichols and His Five Pennies."

Nolla, Olga (1938– 2001): A Puerto Rican poet, novelist, and professor of literature. She published six volumes of poetry, including *El castillo de la memoria* (1996).

Novo, Salvador (1904–74): A Mexican poet who won his country's national prize for literature in 1967.

O'Neill, Hector (1945–): A member of the PNP (New Progressive Party of Puerto Rico) who was elected mayor of Guaynabo in 2004.

Pagán, Bolívar (1897–1961): An historian, journalist, and politician who served in the Puerto Rican Senate from 1933 to 1939.

Palés Matos, Luis (1898–1959): A well-known Puerto Rican poet descended from a family of famous poets. He was best known for reintroducing Africanism into Puerto Rican poetry. He formed the literary movement "Diepalismo" with José I. de Diego Padró.

Pellot Pove, Victor Felipe, a.k.a. "Vic Power" (1927–2005): The second black Puerto Rican to play in Major League Baseball and the first Puerto Rican to play in the American League. He is widely considered to be the greatest Puerto Rican first baseman ever to play the game.

Pérez, Carmín (1929–2003): A heroine of the Nationalist revolt of 1950 and a follower of Pedro Abizu Campos, leader of the Puerto Rican Nationalist movement. She was imprisoned for approximately fifteen years as the result of her participation in the revolt.

Piaf, Édith (1915–63): A beloved singer and national icon of France. She was best known for her heartbreaking ballads such as "La vie en rose" and "Non, je ne regrette rien."

Piranesi, Giovanni Battista (1720–78): An Italian engraver, archaeologist, and architect.

Primo de Rivera, José Antonio (1903–36): A politician and lawyer born into a wealthy family in Madrid, Spain. His father was the military dictator of Spain between 1923 and 1930. Primo de Rivera supported his father's positions and established the Spanish Falange party, calling for a fascist government. Later he supported the military rebellion in July of 1936 that led to the Spanish Civil War. He was captured by the Republicans in 1936, imprisoned, and executed.

Quevedo, Francisco de (1580–1645): One of the most important literary figures of the Spanish Golden Age, known as a poet, satirist, and author of a picaresque novel.

Rexach, Sylvia (1921–61): A poet and songwriter born in Santurce. Though her life was cut short by cancer, many artists continue to perform her poems and songs.

Reyes, Edwin (1946–2001): A Puerto Rican poet, actor, and activist.

Rienzo, Cola di (1313–54): An Italian revolutionary leader who installed himself as dictator of Rome. He was killed by a mob.

Rivera, Danny (1945–): An internationally known singer and songwriter born in Santurce. He is known for such popular songs as "Porque yo te amo," and "Fuiste mia un verano."

Rivera, Ismael (1931–87): A renowned Puerto Rican singer and songwriter, particularly known for his salsa music; nicknamed "El Sonero Mayor."

Rodia, Simon (1879–1965): An Italian masonry worker who lived much of his life in a ghetto of Los Angeles. His most famous creation, the Watts Towers, was a result of a spontaneous vision by a very mysterious man.

Rodríguez, Felipe (1926–96): A Puerto Rican bolero singer. The songs of "La Voz," as he was often known, are considered classics of Puerto Rican music. He had many hit songs including "La última copa," "Golondrina viajera," "Los reyes no llegaron," and "Esta Navidad."

Rodríguez, Tito (1923–73): A popular Puerto Rican singer during the 1950s. Born Pablo Rodríguez Lozada, but known as "The Unforgettable" in part because of his hit song by the same name, he studied music at Juilliard in New York and then went on to become a popular bandleader and musician. He even had his own television show that counted Sammy Davis Jr. and Tony Bennett among others on its guest list.

Romero Barceló, Carlos (1932–): Puerto Rico's fifth democratically elected governor. He was an avid supporter of Puerto Rican statehood.

Ruiz, José: A twentieth-century Puerto Rican artist.

Sábato, Ernesto (1911–): An Argentinean novelist and essayist. His most famous work is, perhaps, *The Tunnel.* He earned a PhD in physics at the Universidad Nacional de la Plata.

Salinas, Pedro (1892–1951): A Spanish poet born in Madrid. As a consequence of the Spanish Civil War, he went into exile in the United States, where he spent a few years at the University of Puerto Rico.

Sánchez, Luis Rafael (1936–): A Puerto Rican novelist and playwright perhaps best known for his novel *Macho Camacho's Beat.* He studied in both the United States and Spain, receiving an MA in dramatic arts from the City University of New York and a PhD in literature from the University of Complutense in Madrid. He is currently a professor emeritus at both the University of Puerto Rico and the City College of New York.

Sánchez Vilella, Roberto (1913–97): The second democratically elected governor of Puerto Rico. He ran for governor in 1964 representing the Popular Democratic Party after Luis Muñoz Marín decided to step down as governor after four terms in office.

Santos Febres, Mayra (1966–): A Puerto Rican writer and professor of literature at the University of Puerto Rico. She received her PhD from Cornell University.

Silva, Myrta (1927–87): A Puerto Rican musician, songwriter, and producer known as the "Queen of the Guarachera." Some of her most famous songs include "Puerto Rico del alma" and "Qué sabes tú."

Soto, Pedro Juan (1928–): A Puerto Rican novelist and professor of literature at the University of Puerto Rico.

Suárez, Miguel Ángel (1939–): A Puerto Rican soap opera and movie actor.

Suau, Gabriel: A Spaniard who immigrated to Puerto Rico and became a well-known TV and film producer.

Szyszlo, Fernando de (1925–): A key figure in advancing abstract Latin American art during the 1950s. He was born in Lima, Peru.

Tapia y Rivera, Alejandro (1827–81): A Puerto Rican writer, poet, dramatist, and historian, considered the father of Puerto Rican letters.

Tego (1972–): Refers to the Puerto Rican rapper Tegui Calderón Rosario, better known as Tego Calderón. His lyrics deal with topics of racism and inequality, as well as the struggles of the poor.

Thomas, Hugh (1931–): A British historian whose book *The Spanish Civil War* was awarded the Somerset Maugham Prize in 1962.

Thompson, Hunter S. (1937–2005): An American journalist and novelist and creator of "gonzo journalism." He was known for his flamboyant writing style. He recorded his experiences in Puerto Rico in the book *The Rum Diary.*

Thurman, Bob "El Múcaro" (1917–98): A baseball player who was famous for hitting homeruns only at night. "Múcaro" refers to a type of owl.

Topo, El. *See* Cabán Vale, Antonio

Torregrosa, José Luis (1917–2001): A Puerto Rican actor, journalist, and cinematographer.

Trías, Arturo (1947–): A Puerto Rican poet who is most famous for his first published volume of poems, *Aunque quise el silencio.*

Trujillo, Rafael Leonidas (1891–1961): The dictator of the Dominican Republic from 1930 until his 1961 assassination. Trujillo legitimized power over his country by passing new constitutions and by winning elections in which he and his party were the only participants.

Tufiño, Rafael (1922–): One of the major figures in twentieth-century Puerto Rican art. He was born in Brooklyn, New York, and known as "the painter of the people."

Ubarri (1823–94): Refers to Count Pablo Ubarri y Capetillo, a Spanish railroad developer and Count of San José de Santurce during the Spanish colonial period.

Umpierre, Tuti (1925–99): A famous guitarist, composer, and bohemian born in San Juan as Rafael Umpierre Hernández. He was the guitar accompanist of famous singer/composer Sylvia Rexach.

Ustáriz, Miguel Antonio de (?–1792): Governed the island of Puerto Rico from 1789 to 1792.

Vallejo, César (1892–1938): A Peruvian poet who spent much time in Europe, having cofounded a cell of the Peruvian Communist Party in Paris. He died in Spain during the Spanish Civil War.

Vate, el. *See* Muñoz Marín, Luis

Vargas Llosa, Mario (1936–): A Peruvian novelist, essayist, playwright, journalist, and literary critic who is one of the most important writers of the twentieth century. Perhaps his most famous novel is *The War of the End of the World.*

Vega, José Luis (1948–): A Puerto Rican poet and critic. He is currently a professor of Latin American poetry at the University of Puerto Rico.

Veray Torregrosa, Amaury (1922–95): A musician from the island of Yauco. His "Villancico Yaucano" is a famous Christmas song.

"Vic Power." *See* Pellot Pove, Victor Felipe

Vigoreaux, Luis (1929–83): A television personality murdered by Papo Newman on January 17, 1983.

Walcott, Derek (1930–): A Caribbean poet and Nobel Prize winner born in Saint Lucia, one of the Lesser Antilles. He divides his time between Trinidad and Boston.

Glossary of Terms

COMPILED BY PETER GRANDBOIS

65th Infantry/65 de Infantería—a military regiment nicknamed "The Borinqueneers." They were an all-volunteer Puerto Rican unit of the U.S. Army who participated in WWI, WWII, and the Korean War. Avenida 65 de Infantería is the name of a famous avenue that links Río Piedras, a San Juan suburb, with the coastal city of Carolina.

936 corporations—the U.S. tax code that allowed U.S. corporations operating in Puerto Rico to repatriate earnings to their stateside parents tax-free.

Alamein, el—one of the most decisive battles in World War II, fought between Montgomery and Rommel in the deserts of North Africa in an area called El Alamein about 150 miles west of Cairo. El Alamein is also the name of a middle-class residential neighborhood off Avenida 65 de Infantería in San Juan.

alcapurrias—beef-filled plaintain fritters.

"Alegria bomba é"—a specific song performed by various artists. *See also* bomba

Animal fiero y tierno—a collection of poetry published by Ángela María Dávila.

bacalaitos—small codfish.

Barrio Camarones—a poor neighborhood in Guaynabo, a city near San Juan.

159

bohío—hut or shack.

Belle Epoque—literally means "beautiful age" and generally used to mean "the golden age." Here, Rodríguez Juliá is referring to a similarity with the French architecture of the period.

bomba—a type of African-influenced music and rhythm developed in Puerto Rico.

Boston Blackie—a character created by Jack Boyle who was featured in a series of mystery movies during the 1920s and 1940s. The films were generally considered B-movies.

brise soleil—literally means "sun breeze."

bucayo—a dicot tree with a red flower. Its scientific name is *Erythria fusca*.

carros públicos—privately owned cars or vans that run along fixed routes supplementing the public bus service. Fares are normally much cheaper than taxis.

Chavales, Los—Spanish musical group popular during the 1950s.

Churumbeles, Los—*See* "Chavales, Los"

Cité Universitaire—literally means "City University."

Coco Rico—a naturally flavored coconut soda from Puerto Rico.

copa—literally means a cup or glass. Rodríguez Juliá draws attention to the fact that the word sounds archaic in Puerto Rican Spanish. Therefore, a more appropriate translation of the word might be "goblet."

criollo—a term that means anything native or traditionally Puerto Rican.

Cuatro Calles—literally means "the four streets."

Danger, Mr.—a character in Rómulo Gallego's novel *Doña Barbara*.

dashiki—a traditional West African men's garment. This colorful garment first became popular in the United States during the civil rights movement of the 1960s.

"Diepalismo"—a literary movement founded by Luis Palés Matos and José I. de Diego Padró. The name "Diepalismo" comes from a combination of the names of its founders. The movement encouraged the use of onomatopoeia and original rhythms.

Don Q—a type of rum made in Puerto Rico.

empanada—a pastry usually stuffed with meat or vegetables.

Estado Libre Asociado (ELA)—Spanish-language equivalent of Puerto Rico's status as a Commonwealth of the United States, as established in 1952; literally means "Associated Free State."

Falangist—a name assigned to several political movements, particularly the original movement in Spain. The Falange in Spain was an authoritarian political organization founded by José Antonio Primo de Rivera in 1933 in opposition to the Second Spanish Republic.

Fania salsa—the music of the Fania All-Stars, established in 1968 as a showcase for the top musicians on the Fania record label. "Fania All-Stars Live at the Cheetah" (1971) became the best selling Latin album produced by one group from one concert ever.

flâneur—a French word first identified by Charles Baudelaire as "a botanist of the sidewalk." It means "stroller," "idler," "loafer," or "lounger."

fufú—See *mofongo*

gámbaros—streets similar to Gámbaro Alley in Old San Juan. These types of streets are narrow, winding, labyrinthine passages.

Georgetti Mansion—designed by the architect Antonín Nechodema and built at a cost of $17 million for Senator Eduardo Georgetti. The mansion was a scene for countless parties and artistic gatherings. It was eventually demolished in 1971.

guayabera—a shirt originating in Cuba in the early 1800s, but now common to all of Latin America and even Spain. It is generally characterized by four frontal pockets and two vertical line decorations, or *alforzas*, running down the front.

Hall of Lost Steps—Rodríguez Juliá is making several allusions here. The Hall of Lost Steps is clearly a reference to Alejo Carpentier's novel *The Lost Steps*, which is in turn a play on André Breton's *Les pas perdus*, which means, interestingly, both "the lost steps," and "the not lost." Further, the capitol in Havana also has a Hall of Lost Steps at its entrance.

hembrismo—perhaps best translated as "femininity" or "essence of womanhood."

jíbaro—used in Puerto Rico to refer to peasants, but its connotations are much broader, as the word has come to refer to "authentic" Puerto Rican people in all their cultural complexity.

lomita—a small humped hill or ridge.

Lopez Sicardo housing project—a public residential area named after Dr. Raphael Lopez Sicardo.

Luxe, calme et volupté—translates as "luxury, calm, and sensual pleasure."

mañanero—a type of fighting cock that crows in the morning.

Marianist—a Catholic religious congregation of brothers and priests, in English called the Society of Mary. The Marianists look to Mary as a model of faith and spirituality.

marímbola—a musical instrument that takes the place of the bass in many Caribbean countries. It is essentially a wood box with several metal "keys" over a sound hole. The keys are played with the thumb.

marquesina—a type of garage, but closer to what we might call a carport.

meaíto—a type of tree known as the "Fire Tree" *(Morella faya)* or "the Flame of the Forest." It is native to West Kenya and Uganda. In Puerto Rico the tree has earned the nickname of *meaíto* because when you squeeze the buds of the tree they release water that smells distinctly like human urine—*meaíto* means "pee."

Miami Windows—also known as "jalousies." These are windows with glass louvers.

Minority Minus One—a radical North American magazine from the sixties.

mofongo—usually fried plantains and pork in the traditional Puerto Rican variety, though it can also be made with shrimp or just about any meat. Although in Cuba *mofongo* is known as "fufú," it is made in essentially the same way.

Morro, El—the *Castillo del Morro.* Located on the northwest tip of Old San Juan, its walls were designed as part of a network of defenses that turned Old San Juan into the "Walled City." Rodríguez Juliá refers to it as the "Campo del Morro."

naif—"naive art," or art that has been created by people without formal training. Artists who have been considered practitioners of naive art include Alfred Wallis, Henri Rousseau, and Grandma Moses.

nueva trova—a type of popular music, translated as "new ballad," that features socio-political protest as its theme.

patria—literally means fatherland, though in Puerto Rico *patria* is used to refer to the island of Puerto Rico itself, while *madre patria* refers to Spain.

petit maître—literally means "little master."

petímetres—the Spanish version of the French *petit maître.*

pieds noirs—literally means "black feet." The term was used to describe people of European descent who lived in North Africa. They were called *pied noirs* because of the black dress shoes they wore. Rodríguez Juliá is using the term to distinguish the American visitors from the native Puerto Ricans.

playita—literally means "little beach."

Plaza Las Américas—known simply as "Plaza" in Puerto Rico. It is the largest shopping mall in the Caribbean. It is located across from the Roberto Clemente Coliseum in San Juan.

Glossary of Terms

plena—a genre of folk music native to Puerto Rico. The *plena* is a narrative song that details the pains and ironies of people and life. "El Bombón de Elena" by Ismael Rivera and Rafael Cortijo is an excellent example of this type of music.

PNP—the Partido Nuevo Progresista, or New Progressive Party of Puerto Rico. It believes in full integration into the United States as the fifty-first state of the Union.

Porfiristas—supporters of Porfirio Díaz, president of Mexico (with the exception of a four-year period) from 1876 to 1911. He was considered a dictator.

reggaeton—a Puerto Rican music style that combines hip-hop, reggae, and salsa or merengue.

Santa Clara—the Puerto Rican name for Hurricane Betsy, which hit Puerto Rico on August 11–12 in 1956.

"to burn petroleum"—an expression from Havana that refers to the fact that almost all of their mistresses were black or mulatto.

todos—in this sense means "everything."

tomateros—agricultural workers who pick tomatoes.

trompe l'oeil—literally means "trick the eye." The term is used to denote an art technique involving realistic imagery in order to create the optical illusion that the depicted objects really exist.

Truman Shirt—also known as an "Aloha" shirt or a "Hawaiian" shirt. It is a short-sleeved shirt generally characterized by brilliantly colored floral or tropical patterns. It is known as a "Truman" shirt because U.S. President Harry S. Truman often wore this type of shirt.

vespertino—a type of fighting cock that crows in the evening.

walk-up—a condominium without an elevator.

Wut—a German word for "anger," "rage," or "blind fury."

Works Cited

Barsy, Kalman. *La cabeza de mi padre*. Valencia: Editorial Pre-Textos, 2002.

———. *Naufragio*. Río Piedras, P.R.: Editorial Plaza Mayor, 1999.

———. *Verano*. Barcelona: Grijalbo-Mondadori, 1995.

Barthes, Roland. *La chambre claire*. Paris: Gallimard, 1980. Translated by Richard Howard as *Camera Lucida* (New York: Hill and Wang, 1981).

Baudelaire, Charles. *The Flowers of Evil*. New York: New Directions, 1958. New edition translated by Keith Waldrop. Middletown, Conn.: Wesleyan University Press, 2006.

Belaval, Emilio S. *Cuentos de la Plaza Fuerte*. 1963. Reprint, Río Piedras, P.R.: Editorial Cultural, 1977.

———. *Los cuentos de la Universidad*. 1935. Reprint, Río Piedras, P.R.: Cultural, 1977.

Curet, José. *Crimen en la calle Tetuán*. San Juan: Editorial de la Universidad de Puerto Rico, 1996.

Diego Padró, José I. de. *Luis Palés Matos y su trasmundo poético*. Río Piedras, P.R.: Ediciones Puerto, 1973.

Echavarría, Arturo. *Como el aire de abril*. San Juan: Editorial de la Universidad de Puerto Rico, 1994.

Ferré, Rosario. *La casa de la laguna*. New York: Vintage, 1996. Translated by Rosario Ferré as *The House on the Lagoon* (New York: Farrar, Straus and Giroux, 1995).

Flax, Hjalmar. *Confines peligrosos.* Madrid: Playor, 1985.

García Ramis, Magali. *Felices Días, Tío Sergio.* Río Piedras, P.R.: Editorial Antillana, 1986. Translated by Carmen C. Esteves as *Happy Days, Uncle Sergio* (Fredonia, N.Y.: White Pine Press, 1995).

González, José Luis. *La luna no era de queso.* San Juan: Editorial Cultural, 1988.

La Torre Lagares, Elidio. *Historia de un dios pequeño.* Río Piedras, P.R.: Editorial Plaza Mayor, 2000.

Mattos Cintrón, Wilfredo. *Desamores.* San Juan: Ediciones de la Sierra, 2001.

Naipaul, V. S. *The Enigma of Arrival.* New York: Vintage, 1988.

Nolla, Olga. *El manuscrito de Miramar.* Mexico City: Alfaguara, 1998.

Palés Matos, Luis. "El llamado." In *Obras 1914–1959,* Vol. 1, edited by Margot Arce de Vásquez. Río Piedras: Editorial de la Universidad de Puerto Rico, 1984.

Rodríguez Juliá, Edgardo. *Cámara secreta.* Caracas: Monte Avila Editores, 1994.

———. *El camino de Yyaloide.* Caracas: Grijalbo, 1994.

———. *Cartagena.* Río Piedras: Editorial Plaza Mayor, 1997.

———. *Cortejos fúnebres.* Río Piedras, P.R.: Editorial Cultural, 1997.

———. *El cruce de la Bahía de Guánica.* Río Piedras, P.R.: Editorial Cultural, 1989.

———. *Elogio de la Fonda.* Madrid: Editorial Plaza Mayor, 2001.

———. *El entierro de Cortijo.* 1983. Reprint, Río Piedras, P.R.: Ediciones Huracán, 1991. Translated by Juan Flores as *Cortijo's Wake* (Durham, N.C.: Duke University Press, 2004).

———. *Mujer con sombrero Panamá.* Barcelona: Mondadori, 2004.

———. *La noche oscura del Niño Avilés.* 1984. Reprint, Río Piedras, P.R.: Editorial de la Universidad de Puerto Rico, 1991.

———. *Puertorriqueños.* Madrid: Editorial Plaza Mayor, 1988.

———. *La renuncia del héroe Baltasar.* 1974. Reprint, Río Piedras, P.R.: Editorial Cultural, 1986. Translated by Andrew Hurley as *The Renunciation* (New York: Four Walls Eight Windows, 1997).

———. *Sol de medianoche.* Barcelona: Mondadori, 1999.

———. *Las tribulaciones de Jonás.* Río Piedras, P.R.: Ediciones Huracán, 1981.

Salinas, Pedro. *El Contemplado.* 1946. Reprint, Madrid: Editorial Castalia, 1996. Translated by Eleanor L. Turnbull as *Sea of San Juan: A Contemplation* (Boston: Humphries, 1950).

Sánchez, Luis Rafael. *La guaracha del Macho Camacho.* 1976. Reprint, Buenos Aires: Ediciones de la Flor, 2004. Translated by Gregory Rabassa as *Macho Camacho's Beat* (Normal, Ill.: Dalkey Archive Press, 2001).

Santos-Febres, Mayra. *Cualquier miércoles soy tuya.* Barcelona: Mondadori, 2002. Translated by James Graham as *Any Wednesday I'm Yours* (New York: Riverhead Books, 2005).

Soto, Pedro Juan. *Ardiente suelo, fría estación.* 1961. Reprint, Río Piedras, P.R.: Editorial Cultural, 1993. Translated by Helen R. Lane as *Hot Land, Cold Season* (New York: Dell, 1973).

Tapia y Rivera, Alejandro. *Mis memorias: O, Puerto Rico cómo lo encontré y cómo lo dejo.* 1928. Reprint, Río Piedras, P.R.: Editorial Edil, 1996.

Thompson, Hunter S. *Fear and Loathing in Las Vegas.* 1971. Reprint, New York: Vintage, 1998.

———. *Rum Diary.* 1998. Reprint, New York: Simon and Schuster, 2003.

Vargas Llosa, Mario. *Conversación en la catedral.* 1969. Reprint, Barcelona: Suma de Letras, 2001. Translated by Gregory Rabassa as *Conversation in the Cathedral* (New York: Harper & Row, 1975; reprint, New York: Rayo, 2005).

Walcott, Derek. *Midsummer.* New York: Farrar, Straus and Giroux, 1984.

Note: With the exception of Barthes's *Camera Lucida,* all excerpts not originally in English translated by Peter Grandbois.

THE AMERICAS

Tent of Miracles
Jorge Amado
Translated by Barbara Shelby Merello; new introduction by Ilan Stavans

Tieta
Jorge Amado
Translated by Barbara Shelby Merello; new introduction by Moacyr Scliar

The Inhabited Woman
Gioconda Belli
Translated by Kathleen March; new foreword by Margaret Randall

Golpes bajos / Low Blows: Instantáneas / Snapshots
Alicia Borinsky
Translated by Cola Franzen and the author; foreword by Michael Wood

A World for Julius: A Novel
Alfredo Bryce Echenique
Translated by Dick Gerdes; new foreword by Julio Ortega

The Mexico City Reader
Edited by Ruben Gallo

Ballad of Another Time: A Novel
José Luis González
Translated by Asa Zatz; introduction by Irene Vilar

The Purple Land
W. H. Hudson
New introduction by Ilan Stavans

A Pan-American Life: Selected Poetry and Prose of Muna Lee
Muna Lee
Edited and with biography by Jonathan Cohen; foreword by Aurora Levins Morales

The Bonjour Gene: A Novel
J. A. Marzán
Introduction by David Huddle

The Decapitated Chicken and Other Stories
Horacio Quiroga
Selected and translated by Margaret Sayers Peden; introduction by Jean Franco

San Juan: Ciudad Soñada
Edgardo Rodríguez Juliá
Introduction by Antonio Skármeta

San Juan: Memoir of a City
Edgardo Rodríguez Juliá
Translated by Peter Grandbois; foreword by Antonio Skármeta

The Centaur in the Garden
Moacyr Scliar
Translated by Margaret A. Neves; new introduction by Ilan Stavans

Preso sin nombre, celda sin número
Jacobo Timerman
Forewords by Arthur Miller and Ariel Dorfman

Prisoner without a Name, Cell without a Number
Jacobo Timerman
Translated by Toby Talbot; new introduction by Ilan Stavans; new foreword by Arthur Miller

Life in the Damn Tropics: A Novel
David Unger
Foreword by Gioconda Belli